JAMES TANNER

take 5
ingredients 5

JAMES TANNER

take 5 ingredients

95 DELICIOUS DISHES USING JUST 5 INGREDIENTS

PHOTOGRAPHY BY

ANDERS SCHØNNEMANN

KYLE BOOKS

I would like to dedicate this book to my daughter Megan.

Big thanks to Kyle Cathie for letting me do the book, Sophie Allen for putting it all together, Nicky Collings for styling and layout, Anders Schønnemann for his great photography, Karen Taylor for food styling, Becca Watson for recipe testing, and Liz Belton for prop styling. My Big Bro Chris Tanner for holding down the fort while we were shooting the pics, Sianypie Lane for typing up all my scribbles, and Big Gav for being Big Gav.

Also all the boys and girls from Tanners Restaurant and Barbican Kitchen who inspire me in their special moments....

Kyle Books
an imprint of Kyle Cathie Limited
www.kylebooks.com
Distributed by National Book Network
4501 Forbes Blvd. Suite 200
Lanham, MD 20706
(800) 462-6420

First published in Great Britain in 2010 by Kyle Cathie Limited

ISBN 978-1-906868-30-7

A cataloging-in-publication record for this title is available from the Library of Congress

10 9 8 7 6 5 4 3 2 1

Design Nicky Collings
Photography Anders Schønnemann
Project Editor Sophie Allen
Food stylist Karen Taylor
Props stylist Liz Belton
Copy editor Stephanie Evans
Production Gemma John

Color reproduction by Sang Choy
Printed by C&C Offset Printing Co.

Contents

INTRODUCTION

Welcome to **Take 5 Ingredients**, a collection of delectable recipes for the home cook, each using just five ingredients in addition to three pantry staples: oil, sea salt, and black pepper. I've included something for everyone and for every occasion, from a quick meal to an elaborate feast, from fish to meat, vegetables to desserts. This collection draws on the dishes I have cooked, served, and eaten in my home, on vacation, and in restaurants that I have worked in, and it is a book that can be used every day to prepare wonderful, inspirational food.

Whenever you are cooking, for yourself or other people, both the cooking and the eating experience should be enjoyable. **Take 5 Ingredients** removes the pressure from shopping for or preparing long lists of ingredients that might be difficult to find or are seldom used, and lets you concentrate on creating great-tasting food without the stress.

If you're already an enthusiastic home cook, I have added some tips to encourage you to experiment: use these recipes and add your own twist. After all, cooking is about being creative with and inspired by ingredients and flavors. Some are pure classics, some are not! I have researched my much-loved favorites and pared them down to create bold, big-flavor food using five ingredients that are easy to buy in your local stores and markets.

My key recommendations when looking for ingredients is to think in terms of quality and seasonality. Try to buy the best you can afford and buy your produce when it's at its best—locally, if possible. Well grown and reared food speaks volumes in flavor, and taste is what it is all about!

So sit back, relax, and choose something you're going to love to cook—you're only 5 ingredients away from a delicious dish!

James Tanner x

Little Dishes

These recipes are fantastic for a light lunch,
brunch, simple snack, or an appetizer.

CHILLED MELON & AVOCADO SOUP

This is a palate-cleansing soup that is refreshing on a hot summer's day. Smooth melon, rich avocado, and zesty citrus teamed with a dollop of crème fraîche and a few raspberries to top it off. Serve this seriously chilled!

Serves 4

1 ripe avocado, **halved and pitted**

1 melon **(galia or cantaloupe)**

1 ¾ cups freshly squeezed orange juice

4 **tablespoons** crème fraîche

12 **ripe** raspberries

Put the avocado halves cut-side down on a flat surface and score the skin with a sharp knife. Peel the skin back to remove. Discard the skin and coarsely chop the avocado.

Cut the melon in half, seed, and scoop out the flesh. Place the melon flesh in a blender or food processor with the avocado and orange juice and blend to a smooth cream. Pass through a fine sieve. Chill the soup for an hour before serving and, at the same time, chill four soup bowls.

Ladle the soup into chilled soup bowls and serve with a rounded teaspoonful of crème fraiche and a sprinkling of raspberries in each bowl.

SPICED PARSNIP SOUP WITH MCINTOSH APPLE

Parsnips, spicy cumin, and tart apple make a great warming combination.

Serves 4

2 **teaspoons** cumin seeds

2 **tablespoons** olive oil

2 onions, **coarsely chopped**

1½lb parsnips, **peeled and sliced**

1 **quart good** chicken stock

crushed sea salt and freshly ground black pepper

1 medium McIntosh apple, **peeled, cored, and grated**

Heat a non-stick frying pan over high heat for 1 minute. Add the cumin seeds. Reduce the heat and dry roast the seeds for 2 minutes until toasted. Remove from the heat and crush using a mortar and pestle.

Heat the olive oil in a large pan, add the onions, and cook for 5 minutes over low heat until softened but not colored. Add the parsnips and crushed cumin seeds. Cover the pan with a lid and cook over low heat for 15 to 20 minutes, stirring occasionally, until the parsnips are just starting to soften.

In a separate pan, bring the chicken stock to a boil. Pour the hot stock over the parsnips and bring to a boil.

Pour into a blender or food processor and blend until smooth (you may have to do this in batches). Season with crushed sea salt and freshly ground black pepper.

When ready to serve, return the soup to a clean pan, stir in the grated apple, and cook over low heat for 3 minutes. Ladle the soup into warmed bowls.

CARROT & CILANTRO SOUP

Fresh carrots, a touch of cilantro—simplicity in a pot.

Serves 4

1 tablespoon olive oil

1 onion, finely chopped

1 teaspoon coriander seeds, crushed

1 lb carrots, peeled and thinly sliced

3 cups vegetable stock (made with bouillon powder)

crushed sea salt

1 cup fresh cilantro, chopped, plus a few leaves for garnish

Heat the olive oil in a large heavy-bottomed pan. Add the onion and coriander seeds, stirring to combine. Cover with a lid and cook over low heat for 5 minutes, stirring occasionally until softened but not colored. Add the carrots, cover, and cook over low heat for another 15 to 20 minutes, stirring occasionally, until just starting to soften.

In a separate pan, bring the vegetable stock to a boil. Pour in the carrots and bring to a boil.

Pour into a blender or food processor and blend until smooth (you may have to do this in batches). Season with crushed sea salt.

When ready to serve, return the soup to a clean pan, stir in the chopped cilantro (reserving a few leaves for garnish), and reheat gently. Ladle the soup into warmed bowls. Top with the reserved cilantro leaves.

FRENCH ONION SOUP

This soup takes some time to cook. The onions need to be cooked slowly to release their natural sugars, but it's well worth the wait. Of course, it is a real classic with the accompaniment of gruyère croûtons.

Serves 4

3 tablespoons butter

2 tablespoons olive oil

2¼ lb onions, thinly sliced

1 bay leaf

small bunch fresh thyme (tied with string), plus extra leaves for garnish

1 quart good beef stock

crushed sea salt and freshly ground black pepper

Heat the butter and olive oil in a large heavy-bottomed pan until the butter has melted. Add the onions, reduce the heat, cover, and gently cook for 20 minutes until softened but not colored. Shake the pan occasionally to prevent the onions from sticking to the bottom.

Increase the heat slightly, add the bay leaf and thyme, and cook, covered, for another 20 minutes until the onions are dark golden, sticky, and caramelized. Stir occasionally to prevent the onions from sticking to the bottom.

Add the stock, stirring with a wooden spoon, scraping the bottom of the pan well. Bring to a boil, reduce the heat, and simmer over very low heat for 20 minutes. Remove the bunch of thyme and discard. Skim off any fat from the top of the pan and season with crushed sea salt and freshly ground black pepper.

Ladle into warmed bowls and garnish with fresh thyme leaves.

WATERCRESS SOUP

This is no ordinary soup. When I was first shown how to make this, it was drilled into me that the soup had to taste fantastic with perfect seasoning but also to be the perfect color. Part of achieving that color is quick cooking—if you are not serving it immediately, you can save the gorgeous bright green by rapidly chilling the soup. The soup can be served hot or cold and is also great served with a poached egg.

Serves 4

2 bunches (9oz) watercress, washed

2 tablespoons olive oil

2 onions, finely chopped

2 garlic cloves, peeled and crushed

1 potato, peeled and thinly sliced

3 cups chicken stock

crushed sea salt and freshly ground black pepper

Pick the stems from the watercress and finely chop. Set aside the watercress leaves. Heat the olive oil in a heavy-bottomed pan. Add the onions and garlic and cook over low heat for 5 minutes, stirring occasionally until softened but not colored. Add the sliced potato and chopped watercress stems to the pan and cook for another 10 minutes until the potatoes are soft.

In a separate pan, bring the chicken stock to a boil. Pour in the potato and onion mixture. Add half the watercress leaves and bring to a boil.

Pour into a blender or food processor with the remaining watercress leaves and blend until smooth (you may have to do this in batches). Season with crushed sea salt and freshly ground black pepper. Pass through a fine sieve into a heatproof bowl set in a bowl of iced water.

When ready to serve, return the soup to a clean pan and reheat gently. Ladle the soup into warmed bowls.

FENNEL, ORANGE, POMEGRANATE & PECORINO SALAD

Such a simple salad with clean, fresh flavors. Great for accompanying a meal eaten in the garden on a warm day.

Serves 4

2 large fennel bulbs, trimmed
4 tablespoons olive oil
juice of 1 lemon
4 large blood oranges, peeled and segmented
5½oz pack of pomegranate seeds or seeds from 4 halved pomegranates
crushed sea salt and freshly ground black pepper
5½oz pecorino

Using a mandolin or sharp knife, slice the fennel very (paper) thinly.

Place the fennel in a bowl, add the olive oil and lemon juice, and toss together.

Add the blood orange segments and pomegranate seeds. Season with crushed sea salt and freshly ground black pepper and toss together.

Arrange the fennel salad on serving plates and use a vegetable peeler to shave the pecorino over the top of each plate.

TIP
To avoid getting that chewy taste of the thin skin (membrane) between each orange segment, remove the peel and then use a small paring knife to cut between the membrane of each segment. They should come away cleanly.

BAKED BEET & GOAT CHEESE STACKS

Beet and goat cheese are great together: the earthy taste of roasted beets marries perfectly with creamy rich goat cheese and the balsamic vinegar in the dressing adds a bit of zing. Serve with lamb's lettuce or mache for a touch of green.

Serves 4

2 tablespoons olive oil, plus extra for oiling

3 large beets, washed but unpeeled

crushed sea salt and freshly ground black pepper

7oz goat cheese (choose a semi-dried log)

⅓ cup heavy whipping cream

1 shallot, finely chopped

1 tablespoon balsamic vinegar

Preheat the oven to 400°F. Oil the beets and place on a large sheet of foil. Sprinkle with crushed sea salt. Gather the edges of the foil together to seal the beets inside. Bake for 1 hour. Remove from the oven, unwrap the foil, and leave the beets to cool.

Crumble the goat cheese into the bowl of a food processor. Season with crushed sea salt and freshly ground black pepper and pulse until blended. Add the whipping cream and process until just smooth. Spoon the goat cheese mixture into a piping bag fitted with a plain nozzle.

Peel the cooled beets and cut into ½-inch slices (you need 4 slices from each beet). Using a 2-inch pastry cutter, cut the beet slices into disks, reserving the trimmings. Pipe a small amount of goat cheese mixture onto the center of four serving plates and top each with a beet disk. Pipe more goat cheese on top of the beet disks and continue layering the beet and goat cheese until you have a stack of 3 disks of beet on each plate.

Chop the reserved beet trimmings and place in a bowl with the shallot.

Stir in the olive oil and balsamic vinegar and season with crushed sea salt and freshly ground black pepper. Drizzle around the beet and goat cheese stacks and serve.

MUSHROOM & GOAT CHEESE PASTRIES

Juicy baked mushrooms, creamy goat cheese, and pungent pesto, finished off with crisp puff pastry make this recipe a real winner!

Serves 4

4 large Portobello
   mushrooms

olive oil, for brushing

crushed sea salt and freshly
   ground black pepper

5½oz goat cheese

4 teaspoons pesto

1 free-range egg yolk, beaten

13oz package ready-rolled
   puff pastry

Preheat the oven to 425°F. Wipe the mushrooms with paper towels, remove the stems, and discard. Oil the caps of the mushrooms and place on a baking sheet, gill-side up. Season with crushed sea salt and freshly ground black pepper.

Crumble the goat cheese into a small bowl and sprinkle some over each mushroom. Spoon 1 teaspoon of pesto on top of the goat cheese.

Unroll the pastry on to a lightly floured surface and lightly roll out to form a 12-inch square. Cut the square into four squares measuring 6in.

Brush the edges of the pastry squares with beaten egg and place one square of pastry, egg-side down, over each mushroom. Press the pastry around and under the mushroom caps to seal.

Score the top of the pastry in a criss-cross pattern. Brush with beaten egg and bake for 16 to 18 minutes until the pastry is golden brown. Remove from the oven and leave to stand for 2 minutes before serving.

TIP
You could fill these pastries with lots of different combinations of flavors. Just make sure the filling isn't too "wet" or the pastry will become soggy.

BAKED CAMEMBERT WITH THYME & GARLIC

This recipe is a favorite of mine on a cold winter's night as it always reminds me of times with friends when we would ski and snowboard all day then sit by a log fire and eat and drink all night. If you don't have maple syrup on hand, use a spoonful of honey instead.

Serves 4

1 x 9oz camembert in its wooden box

1 garlic clove, peeled and sliced into matchsticks

½ teaspoon fresh thyme leaves

1 tablespoon maple syrup

1 small baguette, cut into ½in slices

2 tablespoons olive oil, plus extra for brushing

crushed sea salt

Preheat the oven to 400°F. Remove the camembert from the box and discard any wax paper packaging. Take a 10-inch square of foil and place in the box. Place the camembert inside.

Pierce the top of the camembert with the tip of a knife and push in the slices of garlic. Sprinkle the thyme leaves over the top and drizzle with the maple syrup. Loosely scrunch the foil up over the cheese. Set aside.

Brush two 12-inch square sheets (the size of your baking sheet) of parchment paper with oil. Line a baking sheet with one of the oiled parchment sheets, oil-side up. Spread the slices of baguette over the sheet. Drizzle with olive oil and sprinkle with crushed sea salt. Place the remaining sheet of parchment, oil-side down, over the bread.

Place in the oven with the camembert and cook both for 10 to 12 minutes until the cheese has risen and the bread is crisp. Open up the foil and dip in the hot baguette for a simple snack. Delicious!

ROAST PEARS, BLUE CHEESE FONDUE & WALNUTS

A twist on a fondue using classic ingredients that have been served together for years. This particular recipe works well with a simple green salad.

Serves 4

1 teaspoon olive oil

4 ripe but firm pears (bosc), peeled, cored, and halved

1/3 cup white wine

6oz blue cheese

1 tablespoon blossom honey

1/2 cup walnut pieces, toasted

Preheat the oven to 350°F. Heat the olive oil in a deep non-stick frying pan. Cook the halved pears over medium heat for 2 minutes on each side. Remove from the pan and arrange in an 8-inch square gratin dish.

Add the white wine to the pan that the pears were in. Add the blue cheese and honey and stir over low heat until the cheese has melted to a fondue.

Spoon the blue cheese fondue over the pears and roast in the oven for 15 to 20 minutes until golden and bubbling. Let stand for 2 minutes. Spoon the pears into warmed serving dishes and sprinkle with the toasted walnuts.

TIP

You could use apples instead of pears—try Granny Smith or Braeburn. And of course you can vary the blue cheese as to how strong you like your cheese.

EGGS FLORENTINE

This classic dish reminds me of my college catering days. The recipe is a simple version that can be created in minutes. Make sure your spinach is well washed and dried before cooking and that the eggs are runny when served! Why not serve with an English muffin to create a vegetarian benedict-style dish?

Serves 4

3 tablespoons butter
½lb fresh spinach leaves
crushed sea salt and freshly ground black pepper
4 free-range eggs
½ cup heavy whipping cream
¼ teaspoon freshly grated nutmeg

Preheat the oven to 350°F. Heat the butter in a non-stick frying pan. Add the spinach and sauté for 3 minutes until the spinach is just wilted. Season with crushed sea salt and freshly ground black pepper. Turn onto a cutting board and chop finely. Divide the spinach between 4 ramekin dishes.

Make a small well in the center of the spinach and carefully crack the eggs into the wells. Pour 2 tablespoons of cream over each egg and top with a little freshly grated nutmeg.

Bake in the oven for 10 to 12 minutes, until golden and bubbling. Remove from the oven and leave to stand for 2 minutes. Serve in the ramekins.

EGGS BENEDICT

This dish is an extremely popular and delicious choice for brunch. Use free-range eggs, good-quality ham, butter, and English muffins to really appreciate this all-time global classic.

Serves 4 (Makes 8 halves)

for the hollandaise

2 tablespoons white wine vinegar

5 peppercorns

9oz (2¼ sticks) unsalted butter, **melted and skimmed**

3 large free-range egg yolks

crushed sea salt and freshly ground black pepper

to serve

2 tablespoons white wine vinegar

8 free-range eggs

8 slices smoked ham

2 English muffins, **split**

For the hollandaise, pour the vinegar into a saucepan and add the peppercorns. Bring to a boil and simmer for 2 minutes until reduced by half. Remove from the heat, strain, and set aside.

In a small saucepan warm the melted, skimmed butter. Remove from the heat and set aside.

Place a heatproof mixing bowl over a large pan of simmering water. The bottom of the bowl should not touch the water. Add the egg yolks and reduced vinegar and whisk together with a balloon or electric hand whisk.

Whisk vigorously until the mixture forms a foam, ensuring it doesn't get too hot. (To prevent the sauce from overheating, take it on and off the heat while you whisk, and scrape the sides with a plastic spatula.)

Whisk in a small ladleful of the warmed butter. Repeat until all the butter is incorporated and you have a texture as thick as mayonnaise. Finally, whisk in crushed sea salt and freshly ground black pepper to taste. Remove from the heat and set aside over the pan of hot water.

Bring a large saucepan of water to a boil. Add 2 tablespoons of white wine vinegar. Bring back to a boil and swirl the vinegared water. Poach the eggs by cracking them individually into cups and dropping them into the pan of swirling simmering water. Simmer for 2 to 3 minutes. Remove with a slotted spoon and drain on paper towels.

Toast the muffins and put the halves on warmed serving plates. Place a spoonful of hollandaise on each muffin half. Arrange a piece of ham on top, then top with a poached egg. Spoon over the remaining hollandaise and season with freshly ground black pepper.

POACHED DUCK EGG, ASPARAGUS, MUSHROOM & BACON SALAD

This brunch-style dish is always a winner in my house. Remember to buy local asparagus when in season to get the best flavor, and don't overcook the duck egg!

Serves 4

¼lb asparagus spears, snapped where they break naturally to remove woody ends

1 tablespoon olive oil

crushed sea salt and freshly ground black pepper

3½oz smoked bacon, chopped

2 cups mushrooms (preferably chestnut), wiped and halved

4 duck eggs

handful watercress, washed with leaves picked from the stems

Preheat the oven to 425°F. Place the asparagus spears in a single layer on a small roasting pan. Drizzle with olive oil and sprinkle with salt. Roast for 8 minutes. Remove from the oven and set aside.

In a small non-stick pan, cook the bacon for 4 minutes over high heat until golden. Remove from the pan with a slotted spoon, drain on paper towels, and keep warm. Return the pan to the heat and add the mushrooms. Cook in the fat from the bacon for 4 minutes. Add a teaspoon of olive oil to the pan if there isn't enough fat from the bacon. Remove from the heat and set aside.

Poach the duck eggs by cracking them individually into cups and dropping them into a pan of simmering water. Simmer for 4 minutes. Remove with a slotted spoon and drain on paper towels.

Arrange the asparagus spears on serving plates and top with the poached eggs. Season with freshly ground black pepper. Scatter the bacon pieces, mushrooms, and watercress leaves over the top. Drizzle over any remaining juices from the frying pan.

SCRAMBLED DUCK EGG WITH SMOKED SALMON & CHIVES

Creamy, rich, and velvety. Pick up duck eggs from your local farmer's market or supermarket and team with top-quality smoked salmon.

Serves 4

4 duck eggs
½ cup heavy cream
pinch of crushed sea salt
  and freshly ground black
  pepper
2 tablespoons butter
1 tablespoon fresh chives,
  finely chopped
7oz smoked salmon

Whisk the eggs, cream, and salt together until combined and the mixture formed is of uniform consistency.

Heat a large non-stick frying pan over medium heat for 1 minute. Add the butter and let it melt—don't allow it to burn. Pour in the egg mixture and let it sit for 20 seconds without stirring. Stir with a wooden spoon, lifting and folding it over from the bottom of the pan. Let it sit over the heat for another 10 seconds then stir and fold again.

Repeat until the eggs are softly set and slightly runny in places, then remove from the heat and fold the chives through.

Arrange the smoked salmon on serving plates. Season with freshly ground black pepper. Spoon over the scrambled egg.

MACKEREL & CRÈME FRAÎCHE POTATO SALAD

Really fresh mackerel is a must and new potatoes add great taste. I use crème fraîche in the salad because it works well with the oily, rich mackerel. Serve with lemon wedges for your naughty sixth ingredient!

Serves 4

¾lb new potatoes,
    peeled and cut into 1 cm dice

2 tablespoons crème fraîche

2 shallots, finely chopped

1 tablespoon fresh chives,
    finely chopped

crushed sea salt and freshly
    ground black pepper

1 tablespoon olive oil

4 mackerel fillets, pin-boned

Bring a large saucepan of salted water to a boil. Add the potatoes and boil rapidly over high heat for 3 minutes. Remove from the heat and drain well. Return the potatoes to the pan. Fold in the crème fraîche, shallots, and chives. Season with crushed sea salt and freshly ground black pepper.

Heat the olive oil in a non-stick frying pan. Season the mackerel fillets with crushed sea salt and freshly ground black pepper. Add the mackerel, skin-side down, to the pan and cook over medium heat for 3 minutes. Turn and cook for another 2 minutes. Remove from the heat.

Arrange the seared mackerel fillets on warmed serving plates. Spoon over the potato salad and drizzle with any remaining juices.

MOM'S ROASTED RED PEPPERS & ANCHOVIES

This recipe is from my Mom who is a great home cook. She cooks this dish for Dad in summer and he loves it. Try it for yourselves—either hot or cold.

Serves 4

1 x 2oz can anchovies in oil

4 red bell peppers

crushed sea salt and freshly ground black pepper

16 cherry tomatoes, halved

3 garlic cloves, peeled and thinly sliced

2 sprigs fresh rosemary (leaves picked from the stems and chopped)

Preheat the oven to 400°F. Drain the anchovies through a colander, reserving the oil. Cut the peppers in half lengthwise, right through the stems, and remove the seeds. Brush the peppers with the anchovy oil and place on a baking sheet. Season with crushed sea salt (not too much as the anchovies are very salty) and freshly ground black pepper and roast for 20 minutes, until just tender. Remove from the oven.

Place the cherry tomatoes in a bowl with the sliced garlic and rosemary leaves and toss together. Spoon into the pepper halves. Arrange the anchovy fillets in a criss-cross pattern over the filling and drizzle any remaining anchovy oil over the top.

Bake for 15 to 20 minutes until softened and serve warm, or chill and serve as an antipasti.

SALMON WITH CARAMEL CROÛTONS & CONFIT OF LEMON & ARUGULA

I love this dish: the warm salmon, crisp sweet croûtons, and tangy lemon work so well together. If you don't like salmon you can try the recipe with fresh, sustainably-caught tuna.

Serves 4

for the confit of lemon
2 lemons, peeled
3 tablespoons water
½ cup superfine sugar

for the caramel croûtons
2 x 1in slices white bread, from an unsliced loaf
¾ cup superfine sugar

1 tablespoon olive oil
14oz organic salmon fillet, skin on and scaled
crushed sea salt and freshly ground black pepper
handful arugula

For the confit of lemon, use a small paring knife to cut between the thin skin (membrane) of the lemon to release the segments. Remove any seeds before placing the segments in a bowl. Pour the water into a saucepan, add the sugar, and bring to a boil, stirring until the sugar has dissolved. Pour in the lemon segments and leave to cool.

For the caramel croûtons, slice the crusts off the bread and discard. Cut the bread into 1-inch cubes. Place the sugar in a pan and heat over low heat until the sugar begins to dissolve. Watch it carefully and when it begins to melt, swirl the pan to ensure an even color (do not stir the sugar).

Once it is an even golden color, remove from the heat and toss the bread into the pan. Stir to coat. Using a slotted spoon, remove the caramel croûtons from the pan and transfer onto a sheet of parchment paper to cool.

Heat the oil in a large non-stick frying pan over high heat. Season the salmon with crushed sea salt and freshly ground black pepper. Cut the fillet in half and then divide each piece in half again. Place the salmon fillets in the hot pan, skin-side down, and cook for 4 minutes. Turn and cook for another minute.

Arrange the fish on warmed serving plates with the arugula, caramel croûtons, and confit of lemon slices.

HONEY, LIME & SOY JUMBO SHRIMP WITH BOK CHOI

It's well worth it to find the biggest, juiciest jumbo shrimp you can. This recipe is my idea of the perfect holiday food!

Serves 4

16 large raw jumbo shrimp, peeled and deveined

1 tablespoon soy sauce

2 tablespoons blossom honey

zest and juice of 1 lime

2 teaspoons olive oil

3½oz (2) baby bok choi, sliced

Rinse the shrimp and pat dry with paper towels. Pour the soy sauce into a small saucepan. Add the honey, lime zest, and juice. Bring to a boil, reduce the heat, and simmer over low heat for 4 to 5 minutes until reduced by half and syrupy. Remove from the heat and set aside.

Heat a large wok or non-stick frying pan over high heat for 1 minute. Add the olive oil. Heat for 30 seconds. Add the shrimp and stir-fry over high heat for 15 seconds. Add the soy sauce syrup and stir-fry for another 15 seconds. Add the bok choi and stir-fry for 10 to 20 seconds until the leaves are just wilted (don't overcook the bok choi as its water content will make the sauce too runny). Serve immediately.

SALT & CHILI SQUID

Make sure you use seriously fresh squid. The secret here is to use a good heavy-bottomed non-stick frying pan over high heat to cook the squid really quickly. The salt and chili powder add a kick to the soft squid, but be careful not to overcook it, otherwise it can turn rubbery. Serve with lemon wedges and sweet chili sauce for that perfect combination.

Serves 4

1 lb 2 oz squid, cleaned

2 tablespoons cornstarch

2 tablespoons all-purpose flour

1½ tablespoons hot chili powder

1 tablespoon szechuan peppercorns, dry roasted and crushed

2 tablespoons crushed sea salt

2 cups oil, for deep frying

Rinse the squid thoroughly and dry on paper towels. Slice horizontally into ½-inch rings and set aside.

Place the cornstarch in a mixing bowl with the all-purpose flour, chili powder, crushed peppercorns, and crushed sea salt. Add the squid and toss in the flour mixture.

Half fill a wok or saucepan with oil and heat to 350°F, or until a cube of bread dropped in turns golden in 30 seconds.

Remove the squid from the flour mixture and shake off any excess flour. Plunge half the squid into the hot oil and cook for 45 seconds. Remove from the oil with a slotted spoon and drain on paper towels. Repeat with the remaining squid.

MUSSELS WITH BASIL & CHILE

This is inexpensive and quick to cook and has so much flavor. The rule is if the raw mussels don't close when tapped, don't use them, and if they don't open when cooked, don't eat them!

Serves 4

4½lb mussels, **cleaned and beards removed**

1 tablespoon olive oil

3 red chiles **(bird's eye), finely chopped**

⅓ **cup** dry white wine

½ **cup** heavy whipping cream

large handful fresh basil leaves, **torn**

Scrub the mussels in a large bowl of cold water and discard any that don't close after a sharp tap on the sink. Drain and set aside.

Heat the oil in a pan large enough to hold the mussels, add the chile, and cook over low heat for 2 minutes until soft. Add the mussels and wine. Cover and cook over high heat for 2 minutes or until the shells have opened. Discard any mussels that have not opened.

Pour in the heavy whipping cream and cook over low heat for 2 minutes. Add the basil and stir well. Serve in large warm bowls with rustic bread (see page 162) to mop up the sauce.

TIP
Thai basil would work wonderfully in this dish, so if you can find it, try it!

SCALLOPS WITH CHORIZO, ARUGULA & DILL

Scallops and chorizo are the biggest-selling appetizer we've ever had at our brasserie. I even had complaints from customers when I took the dish off the menu! Try if you can to buy diver scallops that are as fresh as possible.

Serves 4

3½oz chorizo sausage
12 diver scallops,
crushed sea salt and freshly
    ground black pepper
1 tablespoon olive oil
4 teaspoons balsamic glaze
    (bought)
handful arugula, washed
8 sprigs of fresh dill

Preheat the broiler to high. Slice the chorizo into 12 slices, no more than ¼-inch thick. Broil for 3 minutes, turning once, until crisp. Remove from the heat, cover with foil, and set aside.

Season the scallops with crushed sea salt and freshly ground black pepper. Heat the oil in a wide, heavy-bottomed frying pan and cook the scallops over high heat for 40 seconds, turn, and cook for another 40 seconds. Remove from the heat.

Arrange the scallops and chorizo on four serving plates. Drizzle the balsamic glaze and spoon the warm juices from the grill over the top. Sprinkle with the arugula and garnish with dill.

CRAB LINGUINE WITH BASIL, LEMON & CHILE

Crab is an old favorite of mine. This dish has such fresh clean flavors, and is best eaten with fresh crusty bread and a glass of chilled white wine.

Serves 4

⅓ cup olive oil
zest and juice of 1½ lemons
4 red chiles (bird's eye), finely
    chopped
¾lb fresh linguine
9oz white crab meat
large handful fresh
    basil leaves, torn
crushed sea salt and freshly
    ground black pepper

Add the olive oil, lemon zest, and chopped chiles to a small pan and place over low heat until they begin to sizzle. Remove from the heat and set aside.

Bring a large saucepan of salted water to a boil. Add the linguine and cook according to the package instructions (about 7 minutes). Drain well, rinse with boiling water, and set aside.

Add the chile and lemon oil to the pan that the linguine was cooked in. Add the lemon juice and cook over medium heat until sizzling. Return the linguine to the pan and add the crab meat. Toss gently for 1 to 2 minutes to warm the crab through.

Fold in the basil and season with crushed sea salt and freshly ground black pepper. Spoon into warmed serving bowls.

PRESSED CHICKEN & PROSCIUTTO TERRINE

A straightforward terrine. Serve with chutney, piccalilli, or a tangy onion marmalade. A perfect accompaniment would be my rustic bread (see page 162).

Serves 4

3¼lb organic chicken thighs on the bone

1 tablespoon olive oil, plus extra for brushing

2 tablespoons fresh thyme leaves

4 garlic cloves, peeled and crushed

1 tablespoon blossom honey

10 slices prosciutto

crushed sea salt and freshly ground black pepper

Preheat the oven to 375°F. Place the chicken thighs in a roasting pan. Drizzle with the oil, 1 tablespoon of the thyme, and the garlic. Mix together with your hands, then roast for 25 to 30 minutes. Remove from the oven and leave until cool enough to handle. Reserve the pan juices.

Pick the meat from the chicken, discarding the skin and bones. Place the chicken meat in a bowl; add the remaining 1 tablespoon of thyme, the honey, and any juices from the roasting pan. Season with crushed sea salt and freshly ground black pepper. Mix together and leave to cool.

Line a 1lb terrine mold or loaf pan with plastic wrap and brush with oil. Line with slices of prosciutto so that they overlap to cover the base and sides and overhang the edges.

Spoon in the chicken mixture then fold over the prosciutto to encase the terrine. Fold the plastic wrap over and press down gently. Place unopened packs of butter on the top to weigh it down (or whatever you can find) and chill overnight.

To serve, lift the terrine out of the dish, remove the plastic wrap, and carefully slice onto serving plates.

Main Events

Everything from quick mid-week suppers to slow braised dishes and dinner party favorites.

ROAST TURBOT WITH CHANTERELLES

Turbot is the king of the sea. It can be pricey, but cooked well has a wonderful taste and it's so delicate it practically melts in your mouth. If it's difficult to find, monkfish also makes a very good substitute. Teamed with the unique nutty flavor of chanterelle mushrooms, this is one of my favorite recipes.

Serves 4

4 x 5½oz tranches of turbot*
   (thick fillets trimmed
   and boned)

sea salt and freshly ground
   black pepper

1 tablespoon olive oil, plus extra
   for brushing

1½ cups chanterelles (or other
   wild mushrooms)

2 shallots, finely chopped

½ cup red wine

½ cup good chicken stock

* If turbot is hard to find, substitute
with monkfish

Preheat the oven to 350°F. Season the underside of the turbot fillets with sea salt and freshly ground black pepper and brush both sides with oil. Heat an ovenproof frying pan over high heat and sear the turbot for 30 seconds on each side. Transfer the pan to the oven and bake for 8 minutes.

Meanwhile, heat the oil in a non-stick frying pan and cook the chanterelles for 5 minutes. Remove from the pan with a slotted spoon and set aside.

Return the pan to the heat and add the shallots. Cook over low heat for 4 minutes until soft. Add the red wine to the pan. Bring to a boil then simmer until reduced by half. Add the chicken stock and bring back to a simmer. Season with sea salt and freshly ground black pepper.

Arrange the turbot on warmed serving plates. Spoon the chanterelles over the top and drizzle the sauce around the fish.

JOHN DORY WITH BEURRE BLANC

The john dory, or St. Pierre, is a flavorful, sweet-tasting fish that is teamed with a rich classic butter sauce in this recipe. Always use unsalted butter for the sauce as salted will be far too strong. For a cheaper but great alternative to john dory use fillets of hake or cod.

Serves 4

9 tablespoons cold unsalted butter, diced
2 shallots, finely chopped
⅓ cup dry white wine
1 tablespoon white wine vinegar
sea salt and freshly ground black pepper
1 tablespoon olive oil
8 john dory fillets, skinned

Melt 2 tablespoons of the butter in a small non-stick pan. Add the shallots and cook over low heat for 4 minutes until soft. Add the wine and vinegar. Increase the heat and simmer until reduced to about 1 tablespoon (practically nothing).

Whisk the remaining stick of cold butter into the reduction one cube at a time, whisking continuously. The sauce will emulsify and resemble a loose custard. Season with sea salt and freshly ground black pepper.

Remove from the heat and pass through a fine sieve. Set aside at room temperature and warm gently when ready to serve.

Heat the olive oil in a large non-stick frying pan over high heat. Season the john dory fillets with sea salt and freshly ground black pepper. Place the fillets in the hot pan, skin- side down, and cook for 2 minutes. Turn and cook for another minute. Remove from the heat.

Arrange the fish on warmed serving plates. Pour the pan juices over the top and spoon over the butter sauce.

FOIL-WRAPPED BAKED SALMON WITH CHILE, ORANGE, SOY SAUCE & SCALLION

The inspiration for this recipe came from a vacation in Thailand. Cooked on a grill, the dish tastes and smells even better. This method can be used to cook any fish fillets or even whole fish. I have served variations of the dish at our restaurants over the years and it has been extremely popular. Our waitstaff tears open the foil bags at the table and the emerging steam from the dish smells wonderful. I recommend a portion of fresh egg noodles to accompany this—whatever fish you use.

Serves 4

- juice of **6** oranges, plus the zest of **2**
- **2 tablespoons** soy sauce
- **2** red chiles **(bird's eye)**, finely chopped
- **6** scallions, trimmed and sliced
- **4 x 3½oz** organic salmon fillets, **skin on**
- sea salt and freshly ground black pepper
- olive oil for brushing

Pour the orange juice into a bowl with the zest and the soy sauce. Add the chopped chiles and scallions and stir together.

Lay four double-layer 12-inch squares of foil over four shallow bowls and push down into the bowls. Season the salmon fillets with sea salt and freshly ground black pepper.

Place one salmon fillet in the middle of each square of indented foil. Pour the orange mixture over each piece of salmon. Gather up the corners of each foil square and crimp together to form a rough pyramid shape.

Heat two large non-stick frying pans over high heat for 1 minute (if you don't have two frying pans, use a deep baking sheet). Brush the base of the foil pyramids with oil. Place the foil pyramids into the two pans (or baking sheet) and cook for 6 minutes until the pyramids are puffed up and you can hear the contents simmering.

Carefully remove from the pan. To serve, tear open the foil pyramids at the table and let the aroma fill the room.

STEAMED SEA BREAM WITH CRUSHED POTATOES

Sea bream fillets are a cheaper alternative to sea bass but have a similar texture and flavor. They are quick to steam and the sweet carrot and pungent wholegrain mustard create a great sauce that marries really well with the fish—or on its own with pasta for a delicious vegetarian meal.

Serves 4

1 lb 2oz new potatoes, scrubbed but not peeled

5 tablespoons cold unsalted butter, diced

1 tablespoon olive oil

sea salt and freshly ground black pepper

1 cup fresh carrot juice

1 tablespoon wholegrain mustard

4 x 5½oz sea bream fillets

Cut the potatoes into quarters. Bring a large pan of salted water to a boil and add the potatoes. Bring to a boil and simmer for 12 minutes until just cooked. Drain well, return to the pan, and crush with 2 tablespoons of the butter, the olive oil, and salt. Cover and set aside. Keep warm.

Pour the carrot juice into a large non-stick frying pan. Bring to a boil, reduce the heat, and simmer for 4 to 5 minutes until reduced by half. Skim off any foam and discard. Stir in the mustard and whisk in the remaining 3 tablespoons of butter until melted and glossy. Season with sea salt and freshly ground black pepper. Keep warm over low heat.

Half-fill the base of a steamer with water and bring to a boil. Season the sea bream fillets with sea salt and freshly ground black pepper. Wrap each fillet in plastic wrap. Place in the steamer and steam for 4 minutes until cooked.

Arrange the crushed potatoes on warmed serving plates. Unwrap the sea bream, place on top of the potatoes, and spoon the carrot and mustard sauce around the fish.

PLAICE FILLETS WITH PANCETTA & BROWN NUT BUTTER

I love this combination: soft, just-cooked plaice (or flounder) fillets with crispy cured pancetta and rich brown nut butter makes for the perfect meal. Serve with sautéed baby spinach and new potatoes for a seriously good supper!

Serves 4

12 thin slices pancetta

2 tablespoons olive oil

7 tablespoons butter

12 plaice fillets* (about 2½oz each)

juice of 1 lemon

2 tablespoons chopped fresh flat-leaf parsley

sea salt and freshly ground black pepper

* If plaice is hard to find, substitute with flounder

Preheat the broiler. Broil the pancetta for 3 minutes, turning once, until crispy. Remove from the oven and drain on paper towels. Decrease the oven temperature to 275°F.

Heat the oil and 2 tablespoons of the butter in a non-stick frying pan. Season the plaice fillets and cook, skin-side up, for 2 minutes. Turn and cook for another 2 minutes. Remove from the heat, transfer to an ovenproof dish, and place in the oven with the pancetta to keep warm.

In a separate non-stick frying pan, heat the remaining 5 tablespoons of butter over medium heat. When the butter starts to smell nutty and turns golden, add the lemon juice and parsley. Bring back to a boil and remove from the heat. Season with sea salt and freshly ground black pepper.

Arrange the plaice fillets on warmed serving plates. Top with the pancetta and spoon the brown nut butter over the top.

POACHED LEMON SOLE WITH TOMATOES & TAPENADE

This recipe is a toned-down taste of Provence: delicate lemon sole fillets, rich tomatoes, salty tangy tapenade, and fresh basil. It works well served with new potatoes or pasta and, for a more classic touch, add some roast garlic cloves to the sauce before serving.

Serves 4

12 lemon sole fillets, skinned

4½ tablespoons black olive tapenade

1 handful basil leaves, plus extra for garnish

1 cup tomato sauce

½ cup boiling water

⅓ cup green beans, blanched and sliced diagonally

sea salt and freshly ground black pepper

Lay the fillets of sole out flat and spread each one with tapenade paste. Lay the basil leaves over the tapenade and roll up each fillet. Secure the rolled fillets together with toothpicks.

Pour the tomato sauce and boiling water into a large, deep frying pan and bring to a boil. Reduce the heat, add the fish, cover the pan, and poach over medium heat for 2 minutes. Turn the fish and poach for another 2 minutes.

Carefully remove the fish and set aside, keeping warm. Add the green beans to the pan and season with sea salt and freshly ground black pepper. Bring to a boil and cook over high heat for 2 minutes.

Arrange the fish on warmed serving plates. Spoon the sauce around the fish and garnish with torn basil.

BEER BATTERED FISH

This recipe uses vast amounts of fresh yeast that can be purchased from any good bakery or supermarket bakery counter. The finished batter is quite simply amazing and produces the best battered fish ever. Just add fries!

Serves 4

¾ cup lager-style beer

1½ cups all-purpose flour, sifted, plus extra for dusting

½ teaspoon superfine sugar

1⅓ cups fresh yeast

pinch of sea salt

3 cups sunflower or other light cooking oil for deep frying

4 x 7oz fresh white fish fillets, skinned (hake, coley, or line-caught sea bass)

Pour the beer into a mixing bowl. Add the flour, sugar, yeast, and salt. Whisk together to make a smooth, thick batter. Cover with a damp kitchen towel and let rise at room temperature for 30 minutes.

Half-fill a saucepan or wok with oil and heat to 350°F, or until a cube of bread dropped in turns golden in 30 seconds.

Take a fish fillet by its tail end and dust with flour. Dip in the batter and plunge into the hot oil. Repeat with the remaining 3 fish fillets. Cook for 4 minutes, turning after 2 minutes, until golden. Carefully remove with a slotted spoon and drain on paper towels.

Serve with homemade tartar sauce (see page 169).

GUINEA FOWL WITH ONION SOUBISE

A touch of classic French cooking. When you eat it you will understand why the classics are still the best.

Serves 4

1 tablespoon butter

4 free-range guinea fowl
  breasts

sea salt and freshly ground
  black pepper

For the soubise

2 tablespoons butter

1 large onion, finely chopped

½ teaspoon fresh thyme
  leaves

½ cup heavy whipping cream

Preheat the oven to 400°F. Melt the butter in a small pan and use to grease a roasting pan and a sheet of parchment paper, cut to the same size as the roasting pan.

Rub the guinea fowl breasts with sea salt and freshly ground black pepper. Place in the roasting pan and cover with the buttered parchment paper. Roast for 20 minutes.

For the soubise, melt the butter in a non-stick saucepan. Add the onions and stir to coat in the butter. Cover and cook over low heat for 20 minutes, stirring every 5 minutes, until softened but not colored. Add the cream, bring to a boil, and simmer, uncovered, over low heat until the cream has reduced by half. Add the thyme leaves and season with sea salt and freshly ground black pepper.

Remove the guinea fowl from the oven and leave to rest for 3 minutes. To serve, carve the breast and fan out on warmed serving plates. Spoon the onion soubise over the top.

GREEN CURRY

Most people I know love a good green curry. Here is a quick way to curry heaven.

Serves 4

1 tablespoon olive oil

2 tablespoons green curry
    paste

1 lb 10oz free-range, skinless and
    boneless chicken breast,
    cut into chunks

zest and juice of 1 lime

1 ⅓ cups coconut milk

small handful fresh
    cilantro, chopped

Heat the oil in a wok or large frying pan. Add the curry paste and cook over high heat for 1 minute. Add the chicken, lime zest, and coconut milk. Bring to a boil, then reduce the heat and simmer for 15 to 20 minutes until thickened slightly.

Stir in the chopped cilantro and lime juice. Leave to stand for a few minutes to allow the sauce to become creamier before serving. You will taste the true flavors of the curry paste when the sauce is slightly cooler.

STIR-FRIED CHILE CHICKEN

Pressed for time and want to cook something fresh with a bit of a kick? Then try this! It really is a meal in minutes that tastes fantastic and beats any takeout hands down. The ultimate quick chile chicken. Serve with fresh egg noodles or rice.

Serves 4

4 garlic cloves, peeled

2 red chiles (bird's eye), halved

2 tablespoons olive oil

4 skinless, boneless chicken
    fillets, sliced

1 tablespoon soy sauce

large handful fresh basil
    leaves, torn

Place the garlic and the chiles in a mortar with 2 teaspoons of the olive oil and grind with the pestle to a paste.

Heat the remaining olive oil in a wok or a large non-stick frying pan over high heat for 1 minute. Add the garlic-chile paste and stir-fry for 10 seconds.

Add the chicken and stir-fry for another 4 minutes. Add the soy sauce and torn basil and stir-fry for another 1 minute until the basil has wilted. Serve immediately.

THAI ROAST CHICKEN

A roast with a kick! I cook this for my friends when they come over and we watch Formula 1 racing on TV. We always argue about who is the best driver and, as an accompaniment to the meal, we always have a case of ice-cold beer! I usually serve this dish with sesame noodles.

Serves 4

2 red chiles (bird's eye), halved and seeded

½ cup coconut cream

zest and juice of 2 limes, plus 2 limes, sliced

handful fresh cilantro

3¼lb free-range chicken

Preheat the oven to 350°F. Put the chiles and coconut cream in a food processor with the lime zest, lime juice, and cilantro. Blend to a smooth paste.

Loosen the skin at the edge of the cavity of the chicken and push your index and middle fingers underneath to form a pocket. With a sharp knife, slash the thighs twice on both sides.

Push most of the paste into the pocket under the skin and rub the remaining paste into the thighs of the chicken.

Lay the lime slices on the bottom of a roasting pan and sit the chicken on top. Cover with foil and roast for 40 minutes. Remove from the oven, remove the foil, and baste the chicken. Return to the oven, uncovered, and cook for another 30 to 40 minutes, basting occasionally. Remove from the oven and rest for 5 minutes.

Carve the chicken onto warmed serving plates.

GINGER & HOISIN DUCK WITH GLASS NOODLES

Head to a local Chinese supermarket for the ginger in syrup and, while you're there, pick up a package of glass or cellophane noodles to serve this with. Tangy ginger and flavorful hoisin work so well with duck. Make sure you render the duck breasts well when cooking to get that ultimate crispy skin.

Serves 4

4 x 6oz boned duck breast

3 pieces of stem ginger in syrup, **chopped, plus 1 tablespoon of the syrup**

2 tablespoons hoisin sauce

6 scallions, **trimmed and chopped**

7oz dried glass noodles

Prick the duck skin with a fork. Heat a large non-stick frying pan over high heat for 2 minutes. Add the duck breasts, skin-side down, and cook over medium heat for 10 minutes. Spoon off the fat and discard. Turn the duck breast and cook for another 2 minutes. Remove from the heat, cover, and let stand.

Return the pan to the heat. Add the chopped ginger and the syrup and cook over low heat for 1 minute. Increase the heat; add the hoisin and 2 tablespoons of water. Cook for 1 minute. Add the scallions and cook, stirring, for 2 minutes until the onions have wilted. Reduce the heat to very low to keep the sauce warm.

Bring a large pan of salted water to a boil and drop in the glass noodles. Cook for 2 minutes, drain well, and spoon onto warmed serving plates. Slice the duck breast diagonally and arrange over the noodles. Spoon the ginger and hoisin sauce over the top.

ROAST DUCK WITH MAPLE & BLACKBERRIES

A twist on a classic recipe. Try this during blackberry season (end of summer to early autumn) when the berries are at their best.

Serves 4

1 x 3¼lb duck
1 tablespoon olive oil
sea salt and freshly ground
    black pepper
1½ cups blackberries
2 tablespoons maple syrup
3 tablespoons crème de
    cassis (blackcurrant liqueur)
1 cup good chicken stock

Preheat the oven to 400°F. Using a roasting fork or skewer, lightly prick the skin of the duck all over (you don't want to pierce the meat). Place the duck on a wire rack in or over the sink. Bring a pot of water to a boil and pour the boiling water over the duck. Leave to stand for 2 minutes and pat dry with paper towels. Rub the duck with olive oil and sea salt.

Place the duck, breast-side down, on the wire rack set over a heavy-bottomed roasting pan. Roast in the oven for 20 minutes. Remove from the oven and turn the duck, breast-side up. Return to the oven and cook for another 40 minutes. Remove from the oven and set the duck and the rack aside.

Drain all the fat from the roasting pan (reserve the fat for when you want to roast potatoes). Place the pan over high heat, add the blackberries, maple syrup, crème de cassis, and chicken stock and bring to a boil, stirring. Remove from the heat. Return the duck to the pan and set it in the blackberry liquid. Return to the oven and cook for another 15 minutes.

Place the duck on a warm plate. Cover with foil and leave to rest for 15 minutes before carving. To serve, place the roasting pan over medium heat to warm the sauce through. Season to taste with sea salt and freshly ground black pepper. Carve the duck and serve with the blackberry sauce.

POT AU FEU

An easy "all-in-one-pot" method of cooking. Eat this on a cold winter's day. Any remaining broth makes a great soup.

Serves 4

3¼lb (medium) free-range chicken

3 leeks, cut into large chunks

4 carrots, peeled and cut into large chunks

small bunch fresh thyme, tied with string

1¼ quarts hot chicken stock

sea salt and freshly ground black pepper

Preheat the oven to 375°F. Place the chicken in a large casserole dish. Add the leeks, carrots, and thyme. Pour in the chicken stock (there should be enough stock to cover the ingredients).

Cover the casserole dish and put into the oven. Cook for 2 hours. Remove from the oven and discard the bunch of thyme. Season with sea salt and freshly ground black pepper.

Remove the chicken from the casserole and carve the meat—it should fall off the bones. Ladle the vegetables into warmed serving bowls and top with the chicken. Ladle over the stock.

GNOCCHI WITH BACON & PEAS

Gnocchi can be eaten with many things. This is how I love to eat it. Add a few plum tomatoes and a chopped red bell pepper if you're not a fan of peas.

Serves 4

3 large potatoes
1 free-range egg yolk
2 ½ cups all-purpose flour, sifted
7oz smoked bacon lardons or chopped bacon
1 cup peas (defrosted from frozen)
sea salt and freshly ground black pepper

Preheat the oven to 350°F. Place the potatoes on a baking sheet and bake for 1 hour, or until the flesh is fluffy. Cut the potatoes in half, scoop out the flesh, and discard the skins.

Pass the potato through a ricer or wire sieve into a large bowl. Add the egg yolk and flour, a little at a time, and mix together until you have a light dough. Cut the dough into six pieces. Use your hands to roll each piece into a long (about 18-inch) sausage shape then cut each one into ¾-inch pieces. Press each piece over the back of a fork.

Heat a heavy-bottomed frying pan. When hot, dry-fry the lardons for about 5 minutes until golden. Remove the lardons from the pan with a slotted spoon and drain on paper towels. Set the pan aside.

Bring a large saucepan of salted water to a boil. Add the gnocchi and boil for 3 to 4 minutes, until the gnocchi rises to the surface. Remove from the heat, drain well, and set aside.

Return the lardon pan to the heat. Add the gnocchi and toss over high heat in the fat from the lardons for 3 minutes until golden. Add the defrosted peas and cook for another 2 minutes. Return the lardons to the pan and season with sea salt and plenty of freshly ground black pepper. Cook for 1 minute to heat through and serve immediately on warmed plates.

CHORIZO PENNE

Chorizo and sherry vinegar work so well together. With a touch of cream and pasta this becomes a quick and simple treat.

Serves 4

¾lb dried penne

9oz chorizo sausage

1 tablespoon olive oil

2 shallots, finely chopped

2 tablespoons sherry vinegar

½ cup heavy whipping cream

Bring a large saucepan of salted water to a boil. Add the penne and cook according to the package instructions (about 10 minutes).

Slice the chorizo diagonally into thin slices, no thicker than ¼in. Heat the oil in a non-stick pan, add the shallots, and cook over medium heat for 2 minutes to soften. Add the chorizo and cook over high heat for 2 minutes until it begins to release oil. Add the sherry vinegar and cook for 1 minute over high heat, stirring to deglaze the pan. Add the cream, bring to a boil, stirring, and remove from the heat. Season with sea salt and freshly ground black pepper.

Drain the penne. Spoon into warmed serving bowls and pour the chorizo sauce over the top.

TIPS

If you are cooking for your kids and don't want to use chorizo, cook up some good-quality sausages, slice them, and add them before you add the cream.

For a lighter alternative, use half-fat crème fraîche instead of cream.

MOM'S TOAD IN THE HOLE

This reminds me of my childhood. Serve hot, with peas, mashed potatoes, and thick homemade gravy.

Serves 4

8 great quality sausages (pork and spiced apple are good)
1 onion, sliced
sea salt and freshly ground black pepper
2 tablespoons olive oil

for the batter
¾ cup all-purpose flour
pinch of sea salt
2 free-range eggs
1 cup whole milk

Preheat the oven to 425°F. Put the sausages in a medium roasting pan (so they are quite snug). Scatter with the onion, season with sea salt and freshly ground black pepper, and drizzle with the olive oil. Bake in the oven for 10 to 15 minutes until the sausages are beginning to brown and the onions are tinged at the edges.

For the batter, sift the flour into a mixing bowl with the salt. Make a well in the center and crack in the eggs. Beat lightly, then gradually pour in the milk, beating all the time, until you have a smooth batter.

Remove the roasting pan from the oven and pour the batter over the sausages. Return to the oven for another 25 to 30 minutes until the batter is crisp, golden, and well risen. Serve immediately.

GARLIC ROAST PORK TENDERLOIN WITH MAPLE ONIONS

Fillets of pork tenderloin are great on price, low in fat, and cook quickly, and the onions add a sweet and sour flavor that works well with the pork. Serve with seasonal vegetables.

Serves 4

2 x 14oz pork tenderloin fillets

sea salt and freshly ground black pepper

4 garlic cloves, peeled and crushed

2 tablespoons olive oil

2 onions, thinly sliced

2 tablespoons maple syrup

1 teaspoon crushed red pepper flakes

Preheat the oven to 350°F. Using the tip of a sharp knife, remove the sinew from the pork fillets to keep them from curling during cooking. Season the pork with sea salt and freshly ground black pepper. Rub with the crushed garlic.

Heat 1 tablespoon of the olive oil in a non-stick frying pan. Add the pork and cook for 1 minute on each side. Remove from the heat and transfer to a roasting pan. Roast in the oven for 12 to 15 minutes until cooked. Remove from the oven. Cover and leave to rest.

Heat the remaining tablespoon of olive oil in a non-stick frying pan, add the onions, and cook over low heat for 10 minutes until soft. Add the maple syrup and red pepper flakes and continue cooking for another 10 minutes until caramelized.

Cut the pork fillets into medallions and arrange on warmed serving plates. Top with the maple onions.

TIP
This dish works just as well with pork or veal chops.

MERGUEZ SAUSAGES, SAUTÉED POTATOES & AND RED ONION

These North African sausages are packed full of flavor and I love them with the sweet red onions and crisp and soft sautéed potatoes. I have even eaten this combination stuffed into a baguette after a late night out with friends—mmm pass the ketchup!

Serves 4

8 merguez sausages

3 red onions, cut into wedges

1lb 10oz potatoes, peeled and thinly sliced

½ cup olive oil

1 cup red wine (merlot)

2 tablespoons (handful) fresh flat-leaf parsley, chopped

sea salt and freshly ground black pepper

Preheat the oven to 300°F. Heat a large non-stick frying pan over high heat for 1 minute. Add the sausages and cook over medium heat for 10 to 15 minutes until browned and cooked through. Remove from the heat and transfer the sausages to an ovenproof dish. Place in the oven to keep warm.

Return the pan to the heat and add the red onions. Cook in the sausage fat (add a little oil if there is not enough fat) for 10 minutes over low heat until softened. Remove from the heat and set aside.

Bring a large pan of salted water to a boil, add the potatoes, and cook for 3 minutes. Drain well and transfer to a baking sheet lined with paper towels. Leave to cool.

Heat the oil in a large non-stick frying pan until hot. Add the potatoes in a single layer, not too tightly packed. (If your pan isn't large enough, use two, or cook the potatoes in batches). Turn the heat to medium-high, so that the potatoes sizzle and cook for 7 minutes. Turn the potatoes 2 or 3 times during cooking but don't move them until they start to brown underneath.

Remove from the pan with a slotted spoon and drain on paper towels. Sprinkle with sea salt and transfer to the oven to keep warm.

Return the onion pan to the heat. Add the wine, bring to a boil, reduce the heat, and simmer for 7 to 10 minutes until reduced by half. Stir in the chopped parsley and season with sea salt and freshly ground black pepper.

Arrange the sausages on warmed serving plates with the sautéed potatoes and red onions.

PORK CHOPS WITH MCINTOSH APPLE MASH & ONION CONFIT

For this recipe, buy good thick-cut pork chops. Perfect with a sweet onion confit.

Serves 4

5 tablespoons **butter**

2 tablespoons olive oil

1 lb onions, **thinly sliced**

1 large McIntosh apple,
   peeled, cored, and chopped

1 lb 10oz potatoes, peeled and
   cut into chunks

sea salt and freshly ground
   black pepper

4 pork chops

Melt 2 tablespoons of the butter and 1 tablespoon of the oil in a heavy-bottomed saucepan over high heat. When the butter foams, add the onions and stir to coat in the butter and oil. Reduce the heat, cover, and cook over low heat for 20 minutes, shaking the pan from time to time.

Remove the lid from the pan, stir, and increase the heat to medium. Cook for another 15 minutes, stirring occasionally. Increase the heat to high and cook, stirring constantly, for 10 minutes, until the onions are a deep golden brown. Remove from the heat and keep warm.

Preheat the oven to 400°F. Place the apple in an ovenproof casserole, add 1 tablespoon of water, cover, and bake in the oven for 15 minutes until just tender. Remove from the oven and set aside.

Meanwhile, bring a large pan of salted water to a boil, add the potatoes, and boil for 15 to 20 minutes until tender. Drain well and mash with the remaining 3 tablespoons of butter. Season with sea salt and freshly ground black pepper and fold in the cooked apple. Keep warm.

Using a sharp knife, slash the skin of the chops (this will help the chops crisp while cooking) and season with sea salt and freshly ground black pepper. Heat the remaining 1 tablespoon of oil in a large ovenproof frying pan. Add the chops and cook for 1 minute on each side to seal. Transfer the pan to the oven and cook for 8 minutes. Remove from the oven and leave to rest for 2 minutes.

Divide the McIntosh mash between warmed serving plates, top each portion with a chop, and spoon over the onion confit.

HERB & MUSTARD-COATED LAMB RACK

This is one of my all-time favorite dishes. You can buy brioche from your local bakery or supermarket. I recommend cooking this dish with spring lamb for the very best flavor.

Serves 4

2 french-trimmed racks of lamb

sea salt and freshly ground black pepper

1 tablespoon olive oil

2 tablespoons pommery (or other wholegrain) mustard

for the herb crust

1 roll brioche

2 tablespoons (handful) fresh flat-leaf parsley, chopped

1 tablespoon fresh rosemary leaves, chopped

Using a sharp knife, cut away the thick layer of fat on the outside of each rack of lamb, trimming off the thin sinewy layer of meat underneath (this will leave you with a thick meaty fillet and a fatty layer that lies against the bones). Discard the trimmed fat. Season the racks with sea salt and freshly ground black pepper.

For the herb crust, break the brioche into pieces and place in a food processor and process for 30 seconds to reduce it to fine crumbs. Add the parsley and rosemary and process for another 15 seconds. Set aside.

Heat the oil in a large non-stick pan over high heat. Add the lamb racks and cook for 2 minutes on each side. Remove from the pan and leave to rest for 5 minutes.

Preheat the oven to 450°F. Place the racks, skin-side up, on a cutting board and smother with the mustard. Press a generous handful of the herb crust over the racks and transfer to a medium roasting pan. Roast for 10 to 15 minutes, depending on how rare you like your lamb. Cover the bones with foil if browning too quickly.

Remove from the oven, cover, and leave to rest for 5 minutes before slicing and serving.

ROAST LOIN OF LAMB WITH GINGER & SOY SAUCE

An Asian-inspired lamb dish with a subtle flavor. Remember that the marinade contains soy sauce, which is salty, so go easy on the seasoning for this one! I serve this with noodles.

Serves 4

2 x 3¼lb lamb loin, **boned and rolled**

sea salt and freshly ground black pepper

1 tablespoon olive oil

½ **cup** teriyaki marinade

1 tablespoon redcurrant jelly

1 tablespoon dry sherry

1 **in piece** root ginger, peeled and grated

Preheat the oven to 400°F. Pierce the fat side of the lamb all over with the tip of a sharp knife. Season with sea salt and freshly ground black pepper. Rub with olive oil.

Heat a large non-stick frying pan over high heat for 2 minutes. Sear the lamb for 2 minutes on each side. Remove from the heat and transfer onto a wire rack in a heavy-bottomed roasting pan. Roast in the oven for 15 minutes.

Pour the teriyaki marinade into a bowl. Add the redcurrant jelly, sherry, and ginger and stir to a smooth glaze.

Remove the lamb from the oven. Brush half the glaze over the lamb. Return to the oven and roast for another 10 minutes. Brush again with the remaining glaze and roast for another 10 minutes. Remove from the oven, cover lightly with foil, and leave to rest for 10 minutes before carving.

Carve the lamb onto warmed serving plates and pour some juice over the top.

6-HOUR BRAISED LAMB SHOULDER

This really is minimum effort for maximum flavor; I wish all cooking could taste this great with so little effort! After the first 30 minutes of cooking, turn down the heat and relax—the dish takes care of itself. Serve with potato and celery-root mash and some green beans.

Serves 4

4¾lb lamb shoulder

1 tablespoon olive oil

sea salt and freshly ground
    black pepper

12 large shallots, peeled

10 sprigs fresh thyme, plus
    1 tablespoon chopped fresh
    thyme leaves

24 garlic cloves (about 2 bulbs),
    peeled

1¾ cups red wine (merlot is
    good)

Preheat the oven to 400°F. Rub the lamb with olive oil and season with sea salt and freshly ground black pepper.

Place the lamb in a heavy-bottomed roasting pan with the shallots and roast for 30 minutes. Remove from the oven and drain off any fat. Add the thyme sprigs and the garlic. Reduce the oven temperature to 275°F. Return the lamb to the oven. Cover the pan tightly with foil and cook for 4½ hours.

Pour the red wine into a pan and bring to a boil over medium heat. Remove the roasting pan from the oven and pour the red wine over the lamb. Return the lamb to the oven, covered, and cook for another hour.

Remove the lamb from the oven and carefully put the lamb, garlic, and shallots in a warm serving dish. Be careful as the lamb should be just falling off the bone. Cover and set aside to rest.

Place the roasting pan over high heat and heat the wine juices. Skim off any fat and stir in the chopped thyme. Season with sea salt and freshly ground black pepper. Pour the juices over the lamb and serve.

SPICED PRIME RIB

A spice and meat lover's dream. How thick will you carve your slice?

Serves 4

2¼lb piece of free-range prime
   rib, on the bone
4 tablespoons olive oil
2 teaspoons five spice
1½ cups basmati and wild rice
¾lb broccoli
4 tablespoons black bean
   sauce
sea salt

Wipe the beef with damp paper towels. Pour 1 tablespoon of the oil into a small bowl. Add the five spice and mix together. Rub all over the beef. Cover with plastic wrap and marinate for 4 hours in the refrigerator.

Preheat the oven to 400°F. Heat 2 tablespoons of the oil in a non-stick pan over high heat. Add the beef and sear for 30 seconds on all sides. Place the beef in a roasting pan and roast in the oven for 30 to 35 minutes (for medium rare), basting after 15 minutes.

Remove from the oven and place on a large warm dish. Cover with foil and leave to rest for 15 minutes.

Bring a large pan of salted water to a boil. Add the rice and cook according to the package instructions. Drain and rinse with boiling water. Return to the pan. Cover with a double layer of paper towels and put the pan lid back on. Leave to stand.

Heat the remaining 1 tablespoon of oil in a wok or large frying pan. Add the broccoli and stir fry for 3 minutes until tender. Add the black bean sauce and stir fry for another 1 minute.

Carve the beef. Spoon the rice onto warmed serving plates. Arrange the beef and spoon the stir-fried broccoli over the top.

SPOT ON BURGERS

Mix it, cook it, eat it—these burgers are spot on! Serve in floured buns with salad, pickles, and your favorite sauce.

Serves 4

2 tablespoons olive oil

1 medium onion, **finely chopped**

1¼lb lean ground beef

1 free-range egg

1 teaspoon paprika (smoked is good)

2 garlic cloves, **peeled and crushed**

½ teaspoon sea salt and ½ teaspoon freshly ground black pepper

Heat 1 tablespoon of the olive oil in a non-stick pan and cook the onion over medium heat for 2 minutes until softened but not colored. Remove from the heat and set aside to cool.

Break up the ground beef and place in a bowl. Add the egg, paprika, cooled onions, garlic, salt, and pepper. Mix together with your hands.

Divide the mixture into four and shape each piece into a round ball with your hands. Press down to form a burger shape. Place the burgers on a plate, cover with plastic wrap, and chill in the fridge for 10 minutes or until required.

Heat the remaining tablespoon of olive oil in a non-stick pan over medium heat. Add the burgers and cook on one side for 4 minutes. Turn and cook for another 4 minutes (for medium rare). Remove from the heat and drain on paper towels.

BEEF BRAISED IN RED WINE

Slow-braised beef should fall apart as you eat it. This recipe works really well with creamy polenta or more traditionally with herb dumplings.

Serves 4

3 tablespoons all-purpose flour

sea salt and freshly ground
    black pepper

1½lb stewing steak, cubed

3 tablespoons olive oil

2 large onions, cut into wedges

1¼ cups red wine (merlot)

1 cup good beef stock

Add the flour to a mixing bowl and season with sea salt and freshly ground black pepper. Add the steak and toss in the flour to coat.

Heat the olive oil in a casserole pan over high heat. Add the onion wedges and cook for 3 minutes, until just starting to color.

Add the beef to the pan and continue frying until browned. Keep the heat high and stir regularly to prevent burning.

Add the red wine. Bring to a boil, lower the heat, and simmer for 4 minutes until the wine has reduced by half.

Pour in the stock. Bring to a boil, reduce the heat, cover, and simmer gently for 1 to 1½ hours, until the meat is tender. Season to taste with sea salt and freshly ground black pepper. Ladle into warmed serving bowls.

BEEF TENDERLOIN BÉARNAISE

Beef béarnaise is one of my favorites. Buy mature, well-hung marbled beef and rest it well after cooking to produce a truly melt in-the-mouth steak.

Serves 4

for the béarnaise

2 tablespoons white wine vinegar

5 peppercorns, crushed

2 fresh tarragon sprigs, plus 1 tablespoon chopped fresh tarragon leaves

18 tablespoons (2¼ sticks) unsalted butter, **melted and skimmed**

3 large free-range egg yolks

sea salt and freshly ground black pepper

for the steak

1 tablespoon unsalted butter

1 tablespoon olive oil

4 x 6oz beef tenderloin fillets

sea salt

For the béarnaise, pour the vinegar into a saucepan and add the peppercorns and tarragon sprigs. Bring to a boil and simmer for 2 minutes until reduced by half. Remove from the heat, strain, and set aside.

Warm the melted butter in a small saucepan. Remove from the heat and set aside.

Place a heatproof mixing bowl over a large pan of simmering water. The base of the bowl should not be in contact with the water. Add the egg yolks and reduced wine vinegar and whisk together with a balloon or electric hand whisk. Whisk vigorously until the mixture forms a foam, making sure it doesn't get too hot. (To prevent the sauce from overheating, take it on and off the heat while you whisk, scraping around the sides with a plastic spatula).

Whisk in a small ladleful of warmed butter. (Go slowly, so that the sauce base doesn't split, or curdle. If it does split, whisk in a teaspoon of boiling water to bring the sauce base back together.) Repeat until all the butter is incorporated and the sauce has a texture as thick as mayonnaise. Finally, whisk in sea salt and freshly ground black pepper to taste. Stir in the chopped tarragon. Remove from the heat and set over the pan of hot water to keep warm.

To cook the steak, melt the butter and oil in a large non-stick frying pan over medium heat. Season the steak with sea salt, add to the hot pan, and brown on both sides. Cook to the desired stage: 2 to 3 minutes on each side for rare, 3 to 4 minutes on each side for medium, 5 to 6 minutes on each side for well done. Remove from the pan and leave to rest for 5 minutes, keeping warm.

Arrange the steaks on warmed serving plates and spoon over the béarnaise.

Vegetable Delights

Quick, big flavored vegetable dishes for all taste buds! Strict vegetarians can substitute the cheese in some recipes for the pure rennet-free variety.

POTATO GRATIN

A classic that is great on its own, with a green salad, or can be served as an accompaniment to most meat dishes.

Serves 4

1½lb potatoes
1 whole garlic bulb
1 cup heavy whipping cream
small bunch fresh thyme, tied
crushed sea salt and freshly
   ground black pepper
1 cup gruyère, grated

Peel the potatoes and, using a mandolin or very sharp knife, slice the potatoes very thinly. Cut the garlic bulb in half horizontally.

Pour the cream into a large non-stick frying pan. Add the garlic and thyme. Warm the cream over low heat. Add the potatoes, bring to a boil, reduce the heat, and simmer over low heat, uncovered, for 15 to 20 minutes, until the potatoes are soft but still have a little bite.

Preheat the broiler. Remove the halved garlic bulb and the thyme from the pan. Season well with crushed sea salt and freshly ground black pepper. Pour the cream and potatoes into a 9-inch square gratin dish. Sprinkle in the grated gruyère and broil for 2 to 3 minutes until the gruyère is melted, golden, and bubbling. Leave to stand for 2 minutes before serving.

TIP
If you're not a vegetarian, you could add cooked smoked bacon or ham to the gratin before you broil it.

BASIL CRUSHED POTATO CAKE

A simple crispy potato cake with pungent basil. It's wonderful served with crème fraîche. Why not add roast asparagus when it's in season?

Serves 4

1½lb new potatoes,
    scrubbed and cut in half
2 tablespoons olive oil
2 shallots, finely chopped
1 garlic clove, peeled and
    crushed
handful fresh basil leaves, torn
½ cup crème fraîche

Bring a large pan of salted water to a boil. Add the potatoes and cook for 15 minutes until just tender. Drain the potatoes and plunge into a bowl of cold water to halt the cooking process. Drain and set aside.

Heat 1 tablespoon of the oil in a non-stick pan. Add the shallots and cook for 2 minutes until soft. Add the garlic and cook for another minute. Remove from the heat.

Return the potatoes to the pan. Add the shallots and garlic and use the back of a fork to crush each potato against the side of the pan until it just bursts open. Fold in the basil and crème fraîche.

Divide the mixture between four 3 x 1-inch metal chef's rings. Heat the remaining 1 tablespoon of oil in a non-stick frying pan. Add the potato rings and cook over medium heat for 5 minutes. Turn and cook for another 5 minutes. Remove the metal rings and serve on warm plates.

PATATAS BRAVAS

This dish is a taste of one of the many tapas plates I enjoyed in Barcelona, while drinking chilled beer and staying up late with my friends.

Serves 4

1½lb floury potatoes (russet)
⅓ cup olive oil, plus 4 tablespoons
6 ripe tomatoes, seeded and chopped
3 red bird's eye chiles, finely chopped
crushed sea salt
2 teaspoons black sesame seeds

Preheat the oven to 425°F. Peel the potatoes and cut into 1-inch dice.

Heat 2 tablespoons of the olive oil in large heavy-bottomed roasting pan. Add the potatoes and shake them in the hot oil until covered. Place in the oven and cook for 20 to 25 minutes until golden brown. Remove from the oven and drain on paper towels. Keep warm.

Heat 2 tablespoons of olive oil in a non-stick pan. Add the chopped tomatoes and chiles and cook over low heat for 10 minutes until the oil begins to separate from the tomatoes. Remove from the heat, pass through a fine sieve, and set aside to cool.

Transfer the mixture to the bowl of a food processor and with the motor running, add the ⅓ cup oil in a slow steady stream, until you have a glossy texture that resembles mayonnaise. Season with crushed sea salt.

Transfer the hot potatoes into a serving dish and spoon over the tomato chile sauce. Sprinkle with the black sesame seeds.

FAVA BEAN, MINT & PECORINO SALAD

Fresh sweet fava beans and salty pecorino—great to nibble on a warm summer's night.

Serves 4

3½lb fava beans in their shells
   or 1lb frozen fava beans
zest and juice of 1 lemon
small bunch fresh mint
   leaves, chopped
3½oz pecorino (half grated and
   half shaved using a peeler)
3 tablespoons extra virgin olive oil
crushed sea salt and freshly
   ground black pepper
large handful arugula

Shell the fava beans if using fresh. Bring a large pan of salted water to a boil, add the beans, and cook for 3 to 5 minutes until tender but still have bite. Drain, refresh in cold water, and peel off the skins.

Place the beans in a bowl. Add the lemon zest and juice, chopped mint, the grated pecorino, and olive oil. Stir together and season with crushed sea salt and freshly ground black pepper.

Place the arugula in a salad bowl and spoon over the dressed beans. Sprinkle with the pecorino shavings and drizzle with a little olive oil to serve.

SWEET & SOUR LEEKS WITH RICOTTA

It is what it says: sweet and sour. The slightly salty creamy ricotta goes really well with the leeks and makes this dish a winner.

Serves 4

2 tablespoons white wine vinegar

2 tablespoons superfine sugar

1½ cups water

8 small leeks

1 teaspoon red pepper flakes

¾ cup ricotta, **crumbled**

Pour the white wine vinegar into a large pan (large enough to accommodate the leeks whole) and add the sugar and water. Bring to a boil and add the leeks. Bring back to a boil. Reduce the heat, cover, and simmer for 8 minutes until the leeks are soft and tender. Remove from the pan and drain, discarding the liquid.

Preheat the broiler. Using a sharp knife, cut the leeks in half lengthwise and place in a 9-inch square gratin dish. Sprinkle in the red pepper flakes and ricotta. Broil for 3 to 5 minutes until the ricotta is golden and bubbling.

Leave to stand for 2 minutes before serving.

TIP

If you're not vegetarian, this is a great side dish to serve with glazed ham; it works beautifully with the flavors.

LIMA BEAN SALAD

So simple to make and it tastes just great. The freshness of the mint with a chile kick will get your taste buds going!

Serves 4

1 cup dried lima beans, soaked overnight, or 2 x 14oz cans lima beans, drained

juice of 1 large lemon

3 tablespoons olive oil

3 red chiles, (bird's eye) seeded and finely chopped

1 small red onion, finely chopped

crushed sea salt and ground black pepper

20 fresh mint leaves, torn

If using soaked dried beans, drain and rinse well. Bring a large saucepan of water to a boil. Add the beans, bring to a boil, and boil for 10 minutes. Reduce the heat and simmer for 25 to 30 minutes until soft. Remove from the heat, drain well, and leave to cool.

Place the cooled cooked beans or drained canned beans in a bowl and toss with the lemon juice and olive oil. Add the chopped chiles and red onion. Season to taste with crushed sea salt and ground black pepper. Toss gently to mix. Just before serving, add the torn mint leaves.

BUTTERNUT SQUASH & BOK CHOI CURRY

This curry has serious flavor from the spices and sweet butternut squash. Why not experiment with different squashes in the autumn months? Serve with your favorite type of rice and use normal basil if you can't find thai basil.

Serves 4

1 ⅓ cups coconut milk

2 tablespoons yellow curry paste

4½lb butternut squash, peeled and cut into chunks

crushed sea salt

4 baby bok choi, cut into quarters

large handful fresh thai basil leaves

Skim the thick creamy milk from the top of the coconut milk and put it in a large non-stick saucepan. Bring the pan to a boil over high heat and add the curry paste. Cook for 2 minutes, stirring until the coconut and curry paste are combined and sizzling.

Add the remaining coconut milk to the pan with the butternut squash. Bring to a boil, cover, and simmer over low heat for 15 minutes until the squash is tender but not soft. Season to taste with crushed sea salt.

Add the bok choi and simmer for 4 minutes until just wilted. Remove from the heat and stir in the thai basil. Spoon into warmed bowls.

PEPPER POCKETS

I made these once for a vegetarian friend and they have remained a hit as everyone seems to love them—particularly as part of a picnic, as the pockets transport well.

Serves 4

for the filling
2 red bell peppers
1 tablespoon olive oil
7oz (1 bag) fresh spinach, chopped
9oz emmental, cut into ½in cubes
½ cup black olives, pitted and chopped
freshly ground black pepper

for the tortillas
1½ cups self-rising flour, sifted
pinch of crushed sea salt
½ cup boiling water
1 teaspoon olive oil, plus extra for brushing

Preheat the oven to 425°F. Place the whole peppers on a baking sheet and roast for 25 to 30 minutes until the skins are starting to blacken. Remove from the oven, place in a freezer bag, seal, and set aside for 5 minutes (this helps to loosen their skins). Reduce the oven temperature to 350°F.

For the tortillas, sift the flour into a mixing bowl with a pinch of crushed sea salt. Add the water and 1 teaspoon olive oil and mix with your hands to form a soft dough.

Knead for 2 minutes on a lightly floured surface until smooth and elastic. Brush the top of the dough with olive oil, return to the bowl, cover with a clean kitchen towel, and leave to rest for 10 minutes.

For the filling, heat the tablespoon of olive oil in a wok or large non-stick frying pan. Add the spinach and stir fry over medium heat for 4 minutes until wilted. Remove from the heat and drain through a sieve, squeezing out any excess moisture.

Remove the peppers from the freezer bag. Skin, seed, and slice. Set aside.

Divide the dough into 8 pieces and roll into small balls in your hands. On a lightly floured surface, roll each dough ball into a circle roughly 9-inches across. Repeat with the remaining dough to make 8 flour tortillas.

Place the spinach in a large bowl. Add the sliced red pepper, emmental, and olives. Mix together and season with freshly ground black pepper. Divide the spinach mixture into 8 and spoon into the center of the 8 tortillas. Brush the edge of each tortilla with water and fold the edges up around the spinach filling to make a tortilla pocket.

Heat a large grill pan over high heat. Add the tortilla pockets and dry fry for 2 minutes on each side. Transfer to a baking sheet and bake for 12 to 15 minutes until golden.

Remove from the oven and leave to stand for 2 minutes before serving or leave to cool completely if packing for a picnic.

FIG & MOZZARELLA TART

People use the term "match made in heaven," and this recipe is just that! Add a drizzle of honey or maple syrup if you wish to sweeten things up, or if you're feeling really luxurious, a drizzle of truffle honey. You could serve this with fresh, undressed wild arugula for an added peppery flavor.

Serves 4 to 6

13oz package shortcrust pastry
2 large free-range eggs
2 cups grated mozzarella,
   (don't worry if it crumbles)
1 cup ricotta
crushed sea salt and finely ground
   black pepper
5 fresh figs, cut into quarters

Preheat the oven to 400°F. Roll out the pastry and line an 8-inch diameter (and ideally 2-inches deep) tart pan with a removable bottom. Line the pastry with a sheet of parchment paper and fill with baking beans. Bake blind for 20 minutes. Remove from the oven and take out the parchment paper and beans. Reduce the oven temperature to 350°F.

Beat the eggs in a mixing bowl. Add the mozzarella and ricotta and mix to a smooth, creamy consistency. Season with crushed sea salt and freshly ground black pepper.

Pour the mixture into the baked pastry case or shell. Smooth the surface with an offset spatula. Bake for 30 minutes. Remove from the oven and arrange the figs, cut-side up, on the surface. Return to the oven and cook for another 10 minutes until the figs are beginning to brown on the edges.

Remove from the oven and leave to cool on a wire rack. To serve, remove the tart from the pan and cut into slices. Serve at room temperature.

ASPARAGUS & MINT FRITTATA

Make this frittata when asparagus is in season; it tastes amazing. The mint adds a fresh kick.

Serves 4

9oz (about 14 spears) asparagus

crushed sea salt and freshly ground black pepper

6 free-range eggs

½ cup parmesan, **grated**

small bunch fresh mint leaves, picked from the stems and torn

1 tablespoon olive oil

Preheat the oven to 400°F. Remove the woody ends of the asparagus by bending them and snapping where they break naturally. Bring a large pan of salted water to a boil. Add the asparagus, return to a boil, and cook for 3 to 5 minutes until just tender. Drain and season with crushed sea salt and freshly ground black pepper. Set aside.

Break the eggs into a bowl and beat lightly. Add all but 2 tablespoons of the parmesan and the torn mint; season with crushed sea salt and freshly ground black pepper.

Heat the oil in an 8-inch ovenproof frying pan. Add the egg mixture and cook over low heat, loosening the egg from the sides until it is just starting to set (it should be quite runny).

Arrange the asparagus on top, sprinkle with the remaining parmesan, and bake in the oven for 1 minute only. Loosen the frittata from the pan with a spatula and transfer to a warm plate. Cut into wedges to serve.

TIP
When asparagus is out of season, you could use fresh peas or sautéed slices of zucchini.

COUSCOUS SALAD

I had never cooked couscous before I moved to the US in the mid-1990s, and at that time they were crazy about grains. This dish always reminds me of that era but it has a modern-day twist that hits all taste buds. The salad can be made in advance and left for up to 12 hours in the fridge to allow the flavors to blend.

Serves 4

1½ cups couscous

zest and juice of 1½ lemons

1⅔ cups boiling water

1 cup sun-dried tomatoes, chopped

¾ cup black olives, pitted and halved

3 tablespoons extra virgin olive oil

crushed sea salt and freshly ground black pepper

9oz halloumi, sliced medium-thin (just under ¼in)

Place the couscous in a large bowl. Add the lemon zest and juice. Pour in the boiling water. Stir, cover with a clean kitchen towel, and leave to stand for 5 minutes until the lemon liquid is absorbed.

Using a fork, fluff the couscous grains to separate them. Stir in the sun-dried tomatoes, olives, and olive oil. Season well with crushed sea salt and freshly ground black pepper. Mix gently.

Heat a large non-stick grill pan for 1 minute over high heat. Reduce the heat to medium and add the halloumi slices. Dry-fry the halloumi for 2 minutes, turn, and cook on the other side for another 2 minutes until they're golden-brown in parts. Remove from the heat and set aside.

Arrange the halloumi slices over the couscous salad.

BLACK RICE SALAD WITH ROASTED PEPPERS & OLIVES

I use black rice for this recipe—it makes the dish a great alternative to ordinary rice salads. You can find it in Chinese stores or speciality supermarkets.

Serves 4

1 ½ cups black rice

4 yellow bell peppers

2 tablespoons olive oil

1 cup mixed sliced olives in oil (on the deli counter of most supermarkets)

2 tablespoons spiced mango chutney (or plain mango chutney)

1 tablespoon sherry vinegar

crushed sea salt and freshly ground black pepper

Preheat the oven to 425°F. Bring a large pan of salted water to a boil. Add the rice and cook according to the package instructions (about 20 minutes). Drain the rice and rinse with boiling water. Transfer to a mixing bowl and set aside to cool.

Meanwhile, place the whole peppers on a baking sheet and roast for 25 to 30 minutes until the skins are starting to blacken. Remove from the oven, place in a freezer bag, seal, and set aside for 5 minutes (this helps to loosen their skins). When cool enough to handle, remove the peppers from the freezer bag. Skin, seed, and slice.

When the rice has cooled, add the roasted peppers, olive oil, mixed olives including the oil, mango chutney, and sherry vinegar. Stir to mix. Season to taste with crushed sea salt and freshly ground black pepper.

SPICED LENTILS

This lentil recipe works particularly well with oily fish but I have included it in the vegetarian section of this book because it tastes great on its own.

Serves 4

1¾ cups puy lentils, soaked overnight in water

1 tablespoon olive oil

2 garlic cloves, peeled and crushed

2 tablespoons soy sauce

2 tablespoons balsamic vinegar

1 teaspoon worcestershire sauce

crushed sea salt and freshly ground black pepper

Drain the soaked lentils. Bring a large pan of salted water to a boil and add the lentils. Bring to a boil, reduce the heat, cover, and simmer for 30 minutes until cooked (the lentils should be soft). Remove from the heat and drain through a fine sieve. Set aside.

Heat the olive oil in a large non-stick pan over low heat, add the garlic, and cook for 1 minute until softened but not colored. Add the lentils to the pan with the soy sauce, balsamic vinegar, and worcestershire sauce. Cook, stirring, over medium heat for 4 minutes.

Season with crushed sea salt and freshly ground black pepper before serving.

TIP

For the purist vegetarian who doesn't eat Worcestershire sauce, keep this quick recipe to 4 main ingredients!

PEARL BARLEY RISOTTO

This is a twist on the classic risotto. Pearl barley has a great texture and is an economical way of cooking for large numbers. You could try this with slow-cooked red cabbage.

Serves 4

1½ cups pearl barley
1 quart good vegetable stock
3 garlic cloves, peeled and crushed
1 tablespoon olive oil
4 shallots, finely chopped
1½ cups parmesan, grated
freshly ground black pepper

Add the pearl barley to a large saucepan. Cover with water and soak, with the lid on, overnight in the fridge.

Drain the soaked pearl barley and rinse under cold running water. Return to the pan with the vegetable stock and one of the crushed garlic cloves. Bring to a boil, reduce the heat, and simmer for 15 minutes until tender. Drain through a fine sieve, reserving the stock.

Heat the olive oil in a non-stick frying pan. Add the remaining 2 crushed garlic cloves and the shallots. Cook over medium heat for 2 minutes until softened but not colored. Add the pearl barley and stir in the parmesan cheese. Cook, stirring, over low heat for 3 minutes. The mixture will thicken.

Add 4 tablespoons of the reserved stock to loosen the mixture.

Season to taste with freshly ground black pepper before serving.

MUSHROOM & GORGONZOLA RISOTTO

Creamy strong gorgonzola is great in a risotto while the mushrooms add a depth of flavor.

Serves 4

- **1 oz** dried porcini mushrooms
- **2 tablespoons** olive oil
- **1 large** onion, finely sliced
- **3 cups** button mushrooms, cleaned and cut into quarters
- **¾ cup** risotto rice (carnaroli, arborio, or vialone nano)
- **1 cup** gorgonzola cheese, crumbled
- freshly ground black pepper

Place the porcini mushrooms in a bowl. Pour in 2½ cups boiling water and leave to soak and soften for 30 minutes. Drain through a fine sieve, reserving the mushroom liquid for stock. Squeeze any excess liquid out of the porcini and chop finely.

Heat the oil in a shallow saucepan or deep frying pan over medium heat. Add the onion and cook for 5 minutes until softened but not colored. Add the button mushrooms and stir to coat in the oil. Cover the pan with a lid and cook over low heat for 20 minutes, shaking the pan occasionally until the mushrooms release their juices.

Increase the heat, add the rice to the pan, and stir to coat all the grains in oil. Stir in the chopped porcini. Add a quarter of the reserved mushroom liquid and simmer over medium heat, stirring until the rice has absorbed the liquid. Add the same amount of stock again and continue to simmer and stir (the rice will start to become plump and tender). Continue adding the stock slowly, stirring constantly until all the liquid has been absorbed (it should take about 20 minutes). If the rice is undercooked and you have run out of liquid, add a splash of water to the pan.

Remove from the pan and sprinkle the gorgonzola over the top. Cover and leave to stand for 2 minutes until the cheese has melted. Season with freshly ground black pepper. Give the risotto a final stir and serve.

TIP
You can use any soft blue cheese for this recipe—choose your favorite.

MACARONI AND CHEESE

Good old macaroni and cheese! Serve it with a salad and some crusty bread.

Serves 4

3½ cups elbow macaroni

3 tablespoons butter

⅓ cup all-purpose flour

2 cups whole milk

2¼ cups red leicester (or other cheddar cheese), grated

crushed sea salt and freshly ground black pepper

Bring a large pan of salted water to a boil. Add the elbow macaroni. Return to a boil, reduce the heat, and simmer for 10 minutes.

Melt the butter in a large saucepan over medium heat. Add the flour and stir to make a roux. Cook over low heat for 2 minutes. Gradually whisk in the milk a little at a time, whisking between each addition until you have thick, velvety sauce. Bring the mixture to a boil, reduce the heat, then simmer over low heat.

Preheat the broiler. Drain the macaroni well and add it immediately to the sauce. Stir in 1½ cups of the grated cheddar and season with crushed sea salt and freshly ground black pepper.

Pour the mixture into a 10-inch square ovenproof dish and top with the remaining cheddar. Broil for 2 to 3 minutes until the cheese is bubbling and golden. Leave to stand for 2 minutes before serving.

BRUSCHETTA

Great as an appetizer or snack. Use ripe sweet plum tomatoes for the best flavor. Why not use the ciabatta recipe in the bread section?

Serves 4

4 ripe sweet plum tomatoes

½ small red onion, finely chopped

small handful fresh basil leaves, torn

1 tablespoon olive oil, plus extra for drizzling

crushed sea salt and freshly ground black pepper

12 slices ciabatta (sun-dried tomato ciabatta, see page 165)

1 garlic clove, peeled

Coarsely chop the tomatoes and place in a bowl with their juices. Add the onion, basil, and olive oil. Season with crushed sea salt and freshly ground black pepper. Toss together and set aside.

Heat a grill pan over high heat for 1 minute. Add the ciabatta slices and toast lightly for 30 seconds on each side. Remove from the pan.

Rub the toasted ciabatta with the garlic clove and drizzle with olive oil. Spoon the tomato mixture over the ciabatta and serve.

Final Flings

A collection of my all-time favorite dessert recipes—enjoy!

TARTE TATIN

One of the first desserts I ever made in a professional kitchen, this is still one of my top favorites. Serve with vanilla ice cream.

Serves 4 to 6

4 granny smith apples
7 tablespoons unsalted butter
⅓ cup superfine sugar
1 vanilla bean
7 oz package puff pastry

Preheat the oven to 400°F. Take a small paring knife and cut each apple into six wedges. Remove the core and seeds.

Melt the butter in a 10-inch ovenproof non-stick frying pan. Add the sugar and cook over medium heat for 3 minutes until the sugar is at the golden caramel stage. Add the prepared apples and coat in the caramel.

Cut the vanilla bean in half lengthwise and scrape out the seeds with the tip of a knife. Add the seeds to the apples in the pan. Discard the pod. Cook the apples over low heat for 2 minutes.

Roll out the puff pastry on a lightly floured surface until the piece is big enough to cut out a circle 10 inches in diameter. Prick with a fork and place the pastry on top of the apples. Push the edges of the pastry down around the inside edge of the pan.

Bake in the oven for 15 minutes until golden. Remove from the oven and put a large plate on top of the pan. Quickly flip the pan over to release the tarte onto the plate (be careful: the caramel juices are very hot).

TIP
You could use pears, firm peaches, or nectarines for this recipe instead of the apples; you could even make a banana one, just steer clear of fruit that is too soft as it will fall apart and get soggy.

LEMON TART

Clean but rich and fresh, this tart is the perfect way to end a meal. In the late summer months, serve with a sauce made with fruits in season—raspberries or blueberries.

Serves 4 to 6

1 x 8-inch sweet pastry shell **or**
  1 x 10½oz package
  sweet pastry
5 free-range eggs,
  plus **1 egg** white
¾ **cup** superfine sugar
zest and juice of 5 lemons
⅔ **cup** heavy whipping cream

If using packaged sweet pastry, preheat the oven to 400°F. Lightly flour the work surface and roll out the pastry to a 12-inch circle, ¼-inch thick. Use to line a deep-sided, 8-inch loose-bottomed tart pan. Line the pastry with a sheet of parchment paper and fill with baking beans. Bake for 20 minutes. Remove the tart shell from the oven and remove the parchment paper and beans. Reduce the oven temperature (or if you're using a pastry shell, preheat) to 325°F.

Meanwhile, break the eggs into a bowl, add the sugar, lemon zest, and juice and whisk to combine. In a separate bowl, whisk the cream until thick and velvety but not fully whisked. Fold the cream into the lemon mixture.

Pour the mixture into the partially baked pastry case or shell and bake for 35 to 40 minutes or until the filling is set and feels spongy in the center. Leave to cool before serving.

RASPBERRY AND PASSION FRUIT MERINGUE ROULADE

Sweet raspberries, tangy passion fruit, and crisp but gooey meringue... enough said!

Serves 4

4 free-range egg whites
1 cup superfine sugar
1 ¾ cups heavy whipping cream
juice and seeds of **3** passion fruit
½lb raspberries

Preheat the oven to 350°F. Line a jelly roll pan (10 x 12in) with parchment paper.

Place the eggs whites in a bowl and whisk until stiff. Slowly add the sugar, one tablespoon at a time, whisking between each addition, until stiff and glossy.

Spoon the mixture evenly into the lined pan. Bake for 15 minutes until crisp on the outside. Remove from the oven and leave to cool completely.

Lay a sheet of parchment paper on a work surface. Turn the meringue out onto it. Peel off the top layer of parchment paper and discard. Whip the cream until it forms soft peaks then stir in the passion fruit juice.

Spoon the cream over the meringue. Sprinkle over the raspberries and add the passion fruit seeds. Start at one of the shorter ends and roll the meringue up away from you (as you would a jelly roll), using the parchment paper to help you turn it over.

Cut into slices and arrange on serving plates.

HONEY BAKED FIGS

Sweet and tangy, buy just-ripe figs so they cook perfectly. Traditionally served with yogurt and almonds but this dish is also divine with crème fraîche and pistachios.

Serves 4

8 fresh, ripe figs
3 tablespoons honey
½ teaspoon balsamic vinegar
⅔ cup greek yogurt
¼ cup toasted almond slivers

Preheat the oven to 425°F. Lay a large sheet of foil across a roasting pan, allowing enough foil to overlap on all sides of the pan to wrap the figs in a package.

Trim the stems of each fig and cut a cross into the top of each one. Gently squeeze each fig to open it out. Spoon the honey equally over the top of the figs. Wrap the figs in the foil to form a well-sealed package and bake for 10 to 12 minutes.

Unwrap the package and transfer the figs to serving plates. Drizzle with balsamic vinegar. Add a good spoonful of greek yogurt to each fig and sprinkle with toasted almonds. Finally drizzle with the remaining juices and melted honey from the foil.

TIP
You could use peach or nectarine halves for this recipe instead of the figs.

SUMMER BREAD PUDDING

A pure taste of the summer. Use slightly stale bread to soak up the juices and serve with whipped cream... yummy!

Serves 4

1½ gelatin sheets
1¼ cups superfine sugar
5 tablespoons water
1 lb 2oz raspberries
1 lb 2oz blueberries
10 slices white bread, crusts removed

Soak the gelatin sheets in a little cold water for 4 to 5 minutes until soft. Place the sugar in a heavy-bottomed saucepan with the water. Heat gently, stirring, until the sugar dissolves. Add the raspberries and blueberries and cook over low heat for 3 minutes until the juices begin to run. Remove from the heat. Squeeze all the water out of the gelatin sheets and add them to the pan. Stir until the gelatin has dissolved. Set aside.

Cut a circle from one slice of bread to fit the base of a 1-quart pudding basin. Line the sides with seven slices of bread; overlap the slices, leaving no spaces. Spoon in the fruit, reserving 3 tablespoons of the syrup.

Top the fruit with the remaining two slices of bread and spoon over the reserved syrup. Cover with a plate that exactly fits inside the basin. Place a weight on top to press down and chill in the fridge overnight.

To serve, turn onto a plate and slice into wedges.

BLACKBERRY & APPLE CRUMBLE

There is nothing better than sweet but tart fruit with a crumbly top. Serve this with my custard recipe (page 172), of course! For a dinner party, you could serve individual crumbles in small oven-proof containers.

Serves 4

for the filling

2 large McIntosh cooking apples, **peeled, cored, and cut into chunks**

¼ cup superfine sugar

1 tablespoon water

½lb blackberries

for the crumble

1 cup all-purpose flour

6 tablespoons cold butter, **cubed**

⅓ cup superfine sugar

Preheat the oven to 375°F. Place the apples in a heavy-bottomed saucepan with the sugar and water. Cook over low heat for 5 minutes. Add the blackberries, remove from the heat, and spoon into a shallow 8-inch ovenproof dish.

To make the crumble, place the flour in a large bowl and rub in the butter until the mixture resembles fine breadcrumbs. Stir in the sugar.

Sprinkle the crumble mixture over the fruit and bake for 25 to 30 minutes until the crumble is golden and the apple and blackberries are hot. Serve with custard (see page 172) or ice cream.

TIP
You could add toated oats or crushed hazelnuts for a different crumble experience. And feel free to use varying fruits for your crumble bottom.

CARAMELIZED PEACH MILLE-FEUILLE

Crisp puff pastry with warm creamy peaches. Be careful not to overcook the peaches—they should have a slightly firm bite.

Serves 4

13oz package all-butter puff pastry

1 ½ cups superfine sugar

1 ¾ cups whipping cream

2 ripe peaches, pitted, and each cut into 8 wedges

Preheat the oven to 400°F. Roll out the pastry sheet to a 12-inch square with ½-inch thickness. Cut the pastry into 4 neat diagonal sheets. Using the tip of a small, sharp knife, slice the top of your diamonds lightly in a criss-cross pattern. Place on a large baking sheet and bake for 15 minutes until golden. Remove from the oven.

Place the superfine sugar in a heavy-bottomed pan. Heat over low heat until the sugar begins to dissolve. Watch it carefully and when it begins to melt, swirl the pan to ensure an even color, but don't stir. Once it is an even golden color, add 3 tablespoons of the cream and the peaches. Stir to coat the peaches in the creamy caramel. Remove from the heat and set aside.

Whisk the remaining cream until it just holds its shape.

To assemble, slice your pastry diamonds in half lengthwise, then put a teaspoon of cream onto the center of 4 serving plates (to stabilize the pastry) and top with a pastry base at a jaunty angle. Add an eighth of the remaining cream onto the 4 diamond bases, then spoon over 4 peach wedges. Top with the remaining cream. Add a drizzle of the remaining caramel sauce and finish with the diamond lid.

GINGERSNAP & MASCARPONE CHEESECAKE

Gingersnaps are not just for dunking in a cup of tea!

Serves 4

2oz gingersnap cookies
(about **7** cookies)

1 vanilla bean, **seeds scraped out, pod discarded**

¾lb mascarpone

⅔ cup superfine sugar

¾ cup heavy whipping cream

Place the gingersnaps in a food processor and process to the consistency of fine breadcrumbs. Set aside. Line a baking sheet with plastic wrap.

Put the vanilla seeds, mascarpone, superfine sugar, and cream into a bowl and whisk until smooth.

Place four 3 x 1½-inch deep metal chef's rings onto the lined baking sheet. Pipe or spoon the mixture into the rings and smooth off with an offset spatula. Cover with plastic wrap and chill in the fridge for 4 hours until set.

Remove the plastic wrap from the top of the cheesecakes. Spread the cookie crumbs onto a plate and dip the top and bottom of the cheesecakes into the gingersnap crumbs. Heat the sides of the metal rings with a blowtorch or hot cloth and slide the rings off. Transfer the cheesecakes to serving plates.

POACHED PEACHES

There is nothing better than poached peaches with a dollop of mascarpone. They also taste great served with ice cream and chopped nuts. You can use nectarines for this dessert, too.

Serves 4

4 large, ripe peaches
1 ½ cups red wine (merlot)
½ cup brown sugar
1 vanilla bean
4 tablespoons mascarpone

Bring a pot of water to a boil and fill another large bowl with iced water. Place the peaches in a bowl and pour in enough boiling water to cover. Leave for 30 seconds, then remove with a slotted spoon and plunge into the bowl of iced water. Remove from the iced water and slip off the skins.

Pour the wine, brown sugar, and vanilla bean into a pan that will accommodate the peaches snugly. Bring the wine to a boil, add the peaches, cover, and simmer over low heat for 10 to 15 minutes until tender but not soft. Turn the peaches halfway through cooking.

Remove the peaches from the pan and set aside to cool slightly, then cut each in half and remove the pits. Return the pan to the heat and boil the syrup for 8 minutes until reduced by half.

Spoon the peaches into bowls, pour the syrup over the top, and serve each with a spoonful of mascarpone.

CHOCOLATE TRUFFLE PUDDING

Easy and quick to make—a chocolate hit that's fit for any occasion.

Serves 4

6oz good-quality dark chocolate, **minimum 70%** cocoa solids, broken into pieces

6oz milk chocolate, **broken into pieces**

½ teaspoon brandy

¼ teaspoon instant coffee granules

¾ cup heavy whipping cream

Melt the dark and milk chocolate together in a heatproof bowl placed over a saucepan of gently simmering water. Stir until combined. Remove the bowl from the heat and set aside to cool slightly.

Pour the brandy into a very small bowl. Add the coffee and stir until dissolved. Whisk the cream until soft and velvety. (Do not fully whisk.)

Using a large metal spoon, gently fold the cream and the coffee mixture into the cooled, melted chocolate. Spoon the mixture into four ramekins. Chill for 4 to 6 hours.

Remove from the fridge about an hour before serving and serve at room temperature.

CHOCOLATE BAVAROIS

A blast from the past—a pure piece of retro chocolateyness.

Serves 4

oil for greasing

2 gelatin sheets

2 free-range eggs, **separated**

¼ cup superfine sugar

1 ⅓ cups heavy whipping cream

2oz good-quality milk or dark chocolate, **broken into pieces**

Lightly oil 4 x ½-cup soufflé dishes. Soak the gelatin in a little cold water for 4 to 5 minutes until soft.

In a mixing bowl, whisk the egg yolks and sugar together until light and fluffy. Pour ⅔ cup of the cream into a saucepan and bring almost to a boil. Pour the warm cream into the egg mixture, stirring. Pour the mixture into a clean pan and cook over low heat, stirring, until the mixture starts to thicken. Continue to stir gently until the mixture is thick enough to coat the back of the spoon. (Do not allow to boil or the mixture will curdle.)

Squeeze all the water out of the gelatin sheets and add them to the custard mixture. Stir until the gelatin has dissolved.

Pass the custard through a fine sieve into a bowl containing the chocolate pieces. Stir well until the chocolate has melted. Place the bowl in a larger bowl of iced water to cool.

Whisk the remaining cream until they form soft peaks and using a large metal spoon, fold into the chocolate mixture. Whisk the egg whites until they form soft peaks and fold into the chocolate mixture.

Pour the mixture into the prepared soufflé dishes and chill for 3 to 4 hours until set.

To serve, briefly dip the basins in hot water. Carefully loosen the sides of the bavarois and turn onto serving plates.

CHOCOLATE MOLTEN CAKES

This is my all-time favorite recipe; if I see a molten cake on any restaurant dessert menu, I have to order it. A runny center is a must and, for that retro, black forest gâteau taste, serve with vanilla cream and cherries with kirsch.

Serves 4

4½oz good-quality dark chocolate, minimum 70% cocoa solids

9 tablespoons unsalted butter, cut into small pieces, plus extra for greasing

4 free-range eggs

⅓ cup superfine sugar

⅓ cup self-rising flour, plus extra for dusting

Melt the chocolate and butter together in a heatproof bowl placed over a saucepan of gently simmering water. Stir until combined then leave to cool.

Preheat the oven to 350°F. Lightly butter and flour 6 x ½-cup soufflé dishes. Whisk the eggs and sugar together until light and pale and doubled in volume.

Fold the egg mixture into the cooled chocolate. Sift in the flour and, using a large metal spoon, fold until combined.

Spoon the chocolate mixture into the prepared soufflé dishes and bake for 8 to 9 minutes until risen—the key is to have a runny center. Slide a knife around each cake to loosen it and carefully turn onto serving plates.

CHOCOLATE AND ALMOND TORTE

A rich treat that will keep you coming back for more. This tastes delicious with rum raisin ice cream or, if you're feeling a little healthier, a dollop of crème fraîche.

Serves 4 to 6

9oz good-quality dark chocolate, minimum 70% cocoa solids

9oz (2¼ sticks) unsalted butter, cut into small pieces, plus extra for greasing

6 free-range eggs, separated

⅔ cup superfine sugar

½ cup ground almonds

Preheat the oven to 350°F. Lightly grease a 10-inch springform cake pan. Melt the chocolate and butter together in a heatproof bowl placed over a saucepan of gently simmering water. Stir until combined then leave to cool.

Whisk the egg yolks with the sugar until light and fluffy. Gradually pour the melted chocolate into the egg mixture, stirring constantly. Using a large spoon, fold in the ground almonds.

Put the egg whites into a clean dry bowl and whisk until they form stiff peaks. Using a large metal spoon, fold the egg whites into the chocolate mixture until they are just combined. Pour the mixture into the prepared pan and bake for 35 minutes. The torte will be very moist in the middle but resist cooking it for longer.

Remove the torte from the oven and leave to cool completely in the pan.

CUSTARD TART

You either love or hate custard tart. I love it and this recipe always hits the spot. For that ultimate brulée tart, sprinkle with superfine sugar and caramelize the top.

Serves 4 to 6

1 x 8-inch sweet pastry shell
  or 1 x 10½oz package
  sweet pastry
1⅔ cups heavy whipping
  cream
6 egg yolks
¼ cup superfine sugar
½ teaspoon freshly grated
  nutmeg

If using packaged sweet pastry, preheat the oven to 400°F. Lightly flour the work surface and roll out the pastry to a 12-inch circle, ¼-inch thick. Use to line a deep-sided, 8-inch tart pan with a removable bottom.

Line the pastry with a sheet of parchment paper and fill with baking beans. Bake for 20 minutes. Take the tart shell from the oven and remove the parchment paper and beans. Reduce the oven temperature (or if you are using a sweet pastry shell, preheat the oven) to 300°F.

Pour the cream into a pan and bring to a simmer. Remove from the heat and set aside.

In a large bowl, whisk the eggs yolks with the sugar until thick, creamy, and pale in color. Pour the simmered cream over the egg mixture and whisk together. Pass the mixture through a fine sieve into the prepared pastry shell or case. Sprinkle the grated nutmeg over the top of the tart. Bake for 1 hour until just set. The tart should be golden on the top with a slight tremor in the center when you jiggle the pan.

Remove from the oven and leave to cool at room temperature on a wire rack. When cool, chill in the fridge until ready to serve.

CRÈME BRULÉE

A classic set custard with a crisp sugar top. I've adapted my big brother Chris' recipe, and it's the best brulée you will try!

Serves 4

1 large vanilla bean
¾ cup whole milk
5 free-range egg yolks
½ cup superfine sugar, **plus**
   8 tablespoons for the topping
¾ cup heavy whipping cream

Preheat the oven to 225°F. Cut the vanilla bean in half lengthwise and use the tip of a knife to scrape out the seeds into a saucepan. Put the vanilla bean and the milk in the pan. Place over low heat and heat until just simmering. Remove from the heat.

In a bowl, whisk the eggs yolks with the sugar until pale and creamy, then slowly whisk in the warm milk and cream. Pass through a fine sieve and skim off any bubbles from the top.

Place four "sur le plat" dishes (these are shallow, 4-inch diameter dishes with crimped or winged edges) on a baking sheet. Divide the mixture between the four dishes. Place in the oven and cook for 1 hour. Remove from the oven and leave to cool, then chill in the fridge for 2 to 3 hours until set.

Sprinkle 2 tablespoons of superfine sugar over each dish and shake the dish gently to spread the sugar evenly. Using a cook's blowtorch, hold the flame just above the surface and keep moving it around until the sugar is caramelized. Serve when the brulée is firm, or within an hour or two.

TIP
Don't be tempted to use deep ramekins—you need to use shallow dishes for this brulée.

ORANGE PANNA COTTA

So simple to make and quite delicious, especially when served with poached or fresh fruit salad. You can garnish with a little extra orange zest, if you like.

Serves 4

2 gelatin sheets
⅓ **cup** whole milk
1 ⅓ **cups** heavy whipping cream
zest of 1 orange
¼ **cup** superfine sugar

Soak the gelatin sheets in a little cold water for 4 to 5 minutes until soft. Pour the milk into a saucepan with the cream and orange zest and bring to a boil. Remove from the heat and add the sugar. Stir until dissolved.

Squeeze all the water out of the gelatin sheets and add them to the pan. Stir until the gelatin has dissolved. Pass through a fine sieve.

Divide the mixture among four ½ cup dariole molds, ramekins, or teacups and leave to cool. Chill in the fridge for 2 to 3 hours until set.

Dip the molds into hot water for 10 seconds each, then invert onto plates.

TIP
For a minty aftertaste, add 6 fresh mint leaves to the saucepan with the cream and orange zest.

ROASTED HAZELNUT TART

The combination of maple syrup and hazelnuts is really addictive, so be careful not to munch too much of this sweet treat! Serve warm with crème fraîche.

Serves 4

1¾ **cups** hazelnuts

1 x **8-inch** sweet pastry shell
or 1 x 10½oz package sweet pastry

4 **tablesoons** (¼ stick) unsalted butter

3 **large** free-range eggs, lightly beaten

1 **cup** maple syrup

Preheat the oven to 350°F. Place the hazelnuts on a baking sheet and roast for 10 minutes until the skins become crisp and the nuts are beginning to brown. Remove from the oven and turn onto a clean kitchen towel. Rub together in the kitchen towel to loosen and remove the skins (discard the skins). Set aside to cool.

Increase the oven temperature to 400°F. If using a package of sweet pastry, lightly flour the work surface and roll out the pastry to a 12-inch circle, ¼-inch thick. Use to line a fluted, 8-inch tart pan with a removable bottom. Transfer the hazelnuts into the pastry case or shell.

Melt the butter in a pan over low heat. Remove from the heat and beat in the eggs and maple syrup. Pour over the hazelnuts. Bake for 45 minutes until golden. Leave to cool in the pan.

CHOUX PASTRY

Do you like éclairs? Profiteroles? Choux buns? Then this is the perfect recipe for you. Use my crème pâtissière (page 173) as a filling and top with fondant icing or chocolate.

Serves 4, makes 12 choux buns or 8 éclairs

¾ cup water

8 tablespoons (1 stick) butter

1¾ cups all-purpose flour, sifted

5 free-range eggs, lightly beaten

Preheat the oven to 400°F. Line a baking sheet with parchment paper. Pour the water into a saucepan with the butter. Cover the top of the saucepan with plastic wrap and bring to a boil. Remove the plastic wrap and add the flour quickly and all at once.

Remove the pan from the heat and quickly beat the mixture vigorously to a firm paste, stirring continuously. Transfer the mixture to a bowl and leave to cool for 10 minutes.

Beat in the eggs (either by hand or using a mixer) a little at a time, stirring vigorously until the paste is smooth and glossy. Continue adding the egg until you have a soft dropping consistency.

Spoon the mixture into a large piping bag fitted with a plain nozzle and pipe the mixture onto the lined baking sheet as required. For choux buns, pipe the mixture into 2-inch disks or, for éclairs, pipe the mixture into sausage shapes 5 inches in length.

Bake for 25 to 30 minutes until golden brown. Remove from the oven and transfer to a wire rack to cool. Fill the choux pastry with crème pâtissière (see page 173) or vanilla cream. Top with melted chocolate or fondant icing.

THE LIGHTEST SPONGE CAKE WITH RASPBERRIES & CREAM

This sponge cake is seriously light. It's up to you what to sandwich in the middle. As the cake itself is low in fat, I thought I would make up for that by having my favorite filling—raspberries and cream!

Serves 4

vegetable oil, for greasing
4 large free-range eggs,
    separated
¾ cup superfine sugar,
    plus extra for dredging
1¼ cups self-rising flour, sifted
pinch of crushed sea salt
½lb raspberries
½ cup heavy whipping cream

Preheat the oven to 350°F. Grease and line two 8-inch cake pans with parchment paper.

In a mixing bowl, whisk the egg yolks and sugar together until pale and creamy. In a separate bowl, whisk the egg whites until stiff. Whisk the egg whites into the egg yolk mixture.

Fold in the flour in small batches using a large metal spoon. Repeat until all the flour is combined. Fold in the salt.

Divide the mixture between the two lined pans and bake for 20 minutes until well risen and golden. Remove from the oven, turn onto a wire rack, and leave to cool.

For the filling, pass ½ cup of the raspberries through a fine sieve. Set aside. Whip the cream to soft peaks and spread over one of the cooled cakes. Spoon the remaining raspberries over the cream and drizzle with the raspberry purée.

Top with the remaining cooled sponge cake and dredge with superfine sugar. Serve with a cup of coffee or tea!

▶

DOUGHNUTS

Eat these warm and try with different fillings: crème pâtissière, custard, jam, chocolate... I bet you'll be licking your fingers!

Serves 4

2 cups all-purpose flour,
   plus extra for dusting
pinch crushed sea salt
½ cup superfine sugar
2 tablespoons cold butter,
   cut into small pieces
¾oz fresh yeast (from the bakery
   counter in the supermarket)
½ cup warm whole milk
2 cups oil for frying, plus extra
   for greasing

Sift the flour into a mixing bowl with the salt and 3 tablespoons of the sugar. Rub the butter into the dry ingredients until it resembles fine breadcrumbs.

Put the yeast in a separate bowl with the warm milk and mix until the yeast is dissolved. Add the yeast mixture to the dry ingredients and, using your hands, mix to a soft dough. (The dough will seem wet; let it stand for 10 minutes, after which it will have firmed a little.)

Turn the dough onto a lightly floured surface and knead for 5 minutes. Return the dough to the mixing bowl, cover with a damp kitchen towel, and leave to rise in a warm place for 40 minutes until doubled in size.

Punch down the dough. Divide into 16 pieces and roll into small balls. Leave to rise on a lightly floured surface, covered with greased plastic wrap, for 40 minutes until doubled in size.

Heat the oil in a saucepan to 350°F, or until a cube of bread dropped in turns golden in 30 seconds. Add the doughnuts, a few at a time, and deep fry for 2 to 3 minutes, turning occasionally until golden brown. (Make sure the oil is not too hot otherwise the doughnuts will brown in a second and not be cooked inside). Carefully remove the doughnuts with a slotted spoon and drain on paper towels. Continue to cook the rest in batches.

Sprinkle the remaining sugar onto a tray and roll the doughnuts in the sugar until coated. Serve warm.

AFTERNOON SCONES

I have always been a fan of the afternoon snack, so here is a great scone recipe. Just add tea, crème fraîche, and good-quality strawberry jam for the full monty.

Serves 4, makes 12 scones

oil for greasing
3½ cups self-rising flour
3 teaspoons baking powder
pinch of crushed sea salt
5 tablespoons cold butter,
    cut into cubes
¼ cup superfine sugar
⅔ cup whole milk, plus extra
    for brushing

Lightly grease a baking sheet with oil. Sift the flour, baking powder, and salt into a mixing bowl. Add the butter and rub into the flour until it resembles fine breadcrumbs. Stir in the sugar, then add the milk, a little at a time, to form a soft dough.

Lightly knead the dough on a floured surface and roll out to a 1-inch thickness. Using a 2-inch pastry cutter, cut out 8 rounds and place on the greased baking sheet. Chill in the fridge for 20 minutes.

Preheat the oven to 400°F. Brush the tops of the scones with a little milk and bake for 12 to 15 minutes until light and golden brown. Remove from the oven and cool on a wire rack.

TIP
For the perfect cheese scones, replace the ¼ cup sugar with a pinch of sugar and add a handful of good-quality grated cheddar cheese into the mixture.

Breads & Sauces

For my breads, I always use fresh yeast, which is available at the bakery counter of any good supermarket (or ask your local bakery), but remember to keep the yeast in the fridge. There are some all-time sweet and savory classic sauces in here too.

RUSTIC BREAD

I came up with this recipe years ago and still make it today. Serve with dipping bowls of extra virgin olive oil and aged balsamic vinegar.

Makes 1 large family loaf
(approx. 3¼lb)

1 cup water

⅔ cup whole milk

1 tablespoon superfine sugar

1oz fresh yeast

2lb bread flour, sifted,
    plus extra for dusting

1½ tablespoons crushed sea salt,
    plus 1 teaspoon

2 fresh rosemary sprigs

1 tablespoon olive oil

Pour the water and milk into a pan with the sugar and heat just until warm. Add the yeast and stir until dissolved.

Add the flour to a mixing bowl with 1½ tablespoons of the salt. Pour in the yeast mixture. Using your hands, mix to a soft dough. (It may need a little more or less water, depending on how dry your flour is. The dough should be soft, but not sticky. If it is sticky, mix in a little extra flour.)

Turn the dough onto a lightly floured surface and knead for 5 minutes. Return the dough to a floured mixing bowl, cover with a clean kitchen towel, and leave in a warm place to rise for 40 minutes (or at room temperature for 1 hour) until doubled in size. Line a baking sheet with parchment paper.

Punch down the dough and form into a large rectangular shape around 2-inch thick. Place the loaf on the lined baking sheet. Cover with a clean towel and leave in a warm place for 40 minutes (or at room temperature for 1 hour) until doubled in size. Preheat the oven to 400°F.

Using the tips of your fingers, make dents all over the loaf. Pick the leaves off the rosemary sprigs and push into the loaf. Drizzle with the olive oil and sprinkle with the remaining teaspoon of crushed sea salt.

Bake for 30 to 35 minutes until well risen and golden. Turn out and check to see if it is cooked by tapping the bottom; it should sound hollow. Leave to cool on a wire rack.

TANNER'S WHOLE WHEAT BREAD

A delicious easy-to-make whole wheat loaf. Enjoy with good-quality butter or, even better, use to make the ultimate fresh crab sandwich!

Makes 2 x 2lb loaves

1 ½ cups warm water

3 tablespoons olive oil, plus extra
  for greasing

1 oz fresh yeast

3 teaspoons light brown sugar

1 lb bread flour, plus
  extra for dusting

1 lb whole wheat flour

1 teaspoon crushed sea salt

Pour the warm water into a mixing bowl with the olive oil. Add the yeast and sugar and whisk until the sugar has dissolved.

Add both flours to a second mixing bowl with the salt. Pour in the yeast mixture and, using your hands, mix to a soft dough. (It may need a little more or less water, depending on how dry your flour is. The dough should be soft, but not sticky. If it is sticky, mix in a little extra flour.)

Turn the dough onto a lightly floured surface and knead for 10 minutes.

Return the dough to the mixing bowl, cover with a clean kitchen towel, and leave in a warm place to rise for 40 minutes (or at room temperature for 1 hour) until doubled in size. Grease 2 x 2lb loaf pans with olive oil.

Punch down the dough and form into 2 loaves. Place in the greased pans, pressing firmly all around the edges so that the loaves are slightly rounded. Cover with a clean kitchen towel and leave in a warm place for 40 minutes (or at room temperature for 1 hour) until doubled in size. Preheat the oven to 400°F.

Bake the loaves for 35 to 40 minutes, until well risen and golden. Turn out and check to see if they are cooked by tapping on their bottoms; they should sound hollow. Leave to cool on a wire rack.

SUN-DRIED TOMATO CIABATTA

This takes the longest time to make of the breads in this book, but is well worth the wait. Experiment with flavors for this recipe—fresh herbs, pitted olives, marinated artichokes—which you would add at the same time as the tomatoes.

Makes 3 ciabatta loaves

for the starter
½oz fresh yeast
⅔ cup warm water
2¾ cups bread flour,
    plus extra for dusting

for the dough
1⅓ cups warm water
¼ cup warm whole milk
¾oz fresh yeast
4 cups bread flour
4oz (drained weight) sun-dried
    tomatoes, chopped
2 teaspoons salt
3 tablespoons olive oil

For the starter, cream the yeast with 3 tablespoons of the water. Add the flour to a mixing bowl. Gradually mix in the yeast mixture and the remaining water to form a firm dough.

Turn the dough onto a lightly floured surface and knead for 5 minutes until smooth and elastic. Return to the bowl. Cover with lightly oiled plastic wrap and leave in a warm place for 12 to 15 hours, until the dough has risen and started to collapse. Dust three baking sheets with flour.

For the dough, pour the warm water and warm milk into a mixing bowl. Add the yeast and whisk until dissolved. Add the yeast liquid to the starter mixture and mix together. Using your hands, gradually add the flour, lifting the dough as you mix. (This will take about 10 minutes). Add the chopped tomatoes, salt, and olive oil. Cover the bowl with lightly oiled plastic wrap and leave in a warm place to rise for 1 to 1½ hours until doubled in size.

Rub your hands with some flour, transfer one-third of the dough onto a baking sheet, trying to avoid punching down the dough. Shape into a rectangle, 1-inch thick. Dust lightly with flour. Repeat with the remaining dough to make another 2 loaves. Leave in a warm place for 30 minutes.

Preheat the oven to 425°F. Bake the ciabatta for 25 to 30 minutes until golden brown. Slide off the baking sheets and check to see if they are cooked by tapping their bottoms; they should sound hollow. Leave to cool on a wire rack.

TOMATO AND OLIVE BREAD

This bread is great eaten as it is and even tastier when used to make crostini or bruschetta.

Makes 2 x 1lb 10oz loaves

½ cup warm water

3 tablespoons olive oil, plus extra for greasing

1oz fresh yeast

1 tablespoon superfine sugar

2lb bread flour, plus extra for dusting

1 tablespoon crushed sea salt

¾ cup tomato juice

handful pitted black olives

Pour the warm water into a mixing bowl. Add the olive oil, yeast, and sugar and whisk until the yeast has dissolved.

Add the flour to a second mixing bowl with the salt. Pour in the yeast mixture and the tomato juice. Using your hands, mix to a soft dough. (It may need a little more or less water, depending on how dry your flour is. The dough should be soft, but not sticky. If it is sticky, mix in a little extra flour.)

Turn the dough onto a lightly floured surface and knead for 10 minutes, adding the olives a few at a time. Return the dough to the mixing bowl, cover with a clean kitchen towel, and leave in a warm place to rise for 40 minutes (or at room temperature for 1 hour) until doubled in size. Grease 2 x 2lb loaf pans with olive oil, or flour 2 baking sheets.

Punch down the dough and form into 2 loaves. Place in the greased pans or shape and place on the floured baking sheets. Cover with a clean kitchen towel and leave in a warm place for 40 minutes (or at room temperature for 1 hour) until doubled in size. Preheat the oven to 400°F.

Dust the loaves lightly with flour. Bake for 25 to 30 minutes, until well risen and golden. Turn out and check to see if they are cooked by tapping on their bottoms. They should sound hollow. Leave to cool on a wire rack.

FRESH MAYONNAISE

Why buy mayonnaise when this recipe takes minutes to make and tastes great? It is best used immediately, so don't store in the fridge for more than 24 hours.

Makes 1 cup

2 medium free-range egg yolks

1 teaspoon dijon mustard

crushed sea salt and freshly ground black pepper

¾ cup light olive oil

juice of ½ lemon

Sit a large mixing bowl on a kitchen towel to keep it from moving around. Place the egg yolks in the bowl with the mustard, a pinch of sea salt, and freshly ground black pepper.

Using a large balloon whisk or electric hand whisk, whisk the ingredients together. Gradually add the oil in a slow, steady stream, whisking continuously until you have a smooth thick mayonnaise.

Check the seasoning and whisk in the lemon juice.

For a thinner mayonnaise, whisk in a couple of drops of boiling water with the lemon juice.

TARTAR SAUCE

This sauce is perfect with any fish, so use it with my Beer Battered Fish (see page 60)!

Makes 1 cup

1 quantity of mayonnaise (see opposite)

3 tablespoons cornichons (baby gherkins), drained and finely chopped

2 tablespoons capers, drained and finely chopped

1 shallot, finely chopped

3 tablespoons, fresh flat-leaf parsley, chopped

crushed sea salt and freshly ground black pepper

Place the mayonnaise in a mixing bowl. Add the cornichons, capers, shallot, and parsley and mix together. Season to taste with crushed sea salt and freshly ground black pepper.

Serve immediately if using the fresh mayonnaise opposite. If you're using store-bought mayonnaise, store, covered, in the fridge for up to 4 days.

SALSA VERDE

The king of salsas: packed with fresh flavors and it works with just about anything!

Serves 4

large handful fresh flat-
leaf parsley leaves

small handful fresh basil
or mint leaves

zest and juice of 1 lemon

1 garlic clove, **crushed**

3 anchovy fillets, **chopped**

⅓ cup extra virgin olive oil

**crushed sea salt and freshly
ground black pepper**

Wash the parsley, basil or mint leaves, shake, then pat dry with paper towels. Pour the lemon juice and zest into the bowl of a food processor. Add the herbs and blend using the pulse action to make a very coarse paste (don't overprocess).

Add the garlic and anchovies and blend, again using the pulse action to achieve a coarse paste.

With the motor running, gradually add the extra virgin olive oil. Remove from the bowl and transfer into a mixing bowl. Season to taste with crushed sea salt and freshly ground black pepper. Cover with plastic wrap and chill in the fridge until needed. Use within 24 hours.

CUSTARD

The ultimate crème anglaise, this is proper custard, which means it's not thick and gloopy but coats the back of a spoon. It's much easier to make than people think.

Serves 4, makes 2 cups

1 vanilla bean
1⅔ cups whole milk
6 free-range egg yolks
½ cup superfine sugar

Cut the vanilla bean in half lengthwise and use the tip of a knife to scrape out the seeds into a saucepan. Put the vanilla bean and the milk in the pan. Place over low heat until just simmering. Remove from the heat and set aside.

Whisk the eggs yolks with the sugar until light and creamy. Pour the warm milk over the egg mixture, stirring. Pour the mixture into a clean pan and cook over very low heat, stirring constantly, until the mixture starts to thicken. (Be careful not to let the mixture boil or it will split.) Stir gently until the mixture is thick enough to coat the back of the spoon. Remove from the heat and pass through a fine sieve.

Pour the custard into a pitcher or bowl to serve.

CRÈME PÂTISSIÈRE

Crème pâtissière is simply French pastry cream: thick, rich, and creamy.
It's a useful filling for many sweet pastries, such as choux pastry, mille-feuille,
doughnuts, and Danishes.

Serves 4, makes 2 cups

1 vanilla bean
2 cups whole milk
6 free-range egg yolks
⅓ **cup** superfine sugar
⅓ **cup** all-purpose flour

Cut the vanilla bean in half lengthwise and use the tip of a knife to scrape
out the seeds into a saucepan. Put the vanilla bean and the milk in the pan.
Place over low heat and heat until just simmering. Remove from the heat
and set aside.

Whisk the eggs yolks with the sugar until light and creamy. Pour the warm
milk over the egg mixture, stirring. Pour the mixture into a clean pan and
cook over low heat for 4 to 5 minutes, whisking, until the mixture starts to
thicken and the whisk leaves a trail in the custard (the mixture should be thick
and the flour taste cooked out).

Remove from the heat and pass through a fine sieve before serving. If you're
not using immediately, cover the surface with plastic wrap to keep a skin
from forming. Cool to room temperature and store in the fridge for up to
48 hours.

INDEX